Cultivating Joyful Learning Spaces for BLACK GIRLS

cultivating
Joyful Learning spaces
for BLACK GIRLS
Insights into Interrupting School Pushout

MONIQUE W. MORRIS

 ascd | Arlington, Virginia USA

2800 Shirlington Road, Suite 1001 • Arlington, VA 22206 USA
Phone: 800-933-2723 or 703-578-9600 • Fax: 703-575-5400
Website: www.ascd.org • Email: member@ascd.org
Author guidelines: www.ascd.org/write

Penny Reinart, *Chief Impact Officer;* Genny Ostertag, *Managing Director, Book Acquisitions & Editing;* Susan Hills, *Senior Acquisitions Editor;* Julie Houtz, *Director, Book Editing;* Liz Wegner, *Editor;* Thomas Lytle, *Creative Director;* Donald Ely, *Art Director;* Georgia Park, *Senior Graphic Designer;* Lisa Hill, *Graphic Designer;* Keith Demmons, *Senior Production Designer;* Kelly Marshall, *Production Manager;* Shajuan Martin, *E-Publishing Specialist;* Christopher Logan, *Senior Production Specialist*

Author photo taken by Roger Archer/ Phaats Photos.

All web links in this book are correct as of the publication date below but may have become inactive or otherwise modified since that time. If you notice a deactivated or changed link, please email books@ascd.org with the words "Link Update" in the subject line. In your message, please specify the web link, the book title, and the page number on which the link appears.

PAPERBACK ISBN: 978-1-4166-3122-4   ASCD product #121004 n6/22
PDF E-BOOK ISBN: 978-1-4166-3123-1; see Books in Print for other formats.
Quantity discounts are available: email programteam@ascd.org or call 800-933-2723, ext. 5773, or 703-575-5773. For desk copies, go to www.ascd.org/deskcopy.

Library of Congress Cataloging-in-Publication Data
Names: Morris, Monique W., 1972- author.
Title: Cultivating joyful learning spaces for Black girls : insights into interrupting school pushout / Monique W. Morris.
Description: Arlington, Virginia : ASCD, 2022. | Includes bibliographical references and index.
Identifiers: LCCN 2022002038 (print) | LCCN 2022002039 (ebook) | ISBN 9781416631224 (paperback) | ISBN 9781416631231 (pdf)
Subjects: LCSH: African American girls--Education. | Academic achievement--United States. | School environment--United States.
Classification: LCC LC2731 .M588 2022 (print) | LCC LC2731 (ebook) | DDC 371.829/96073--dc23/eng/20220302
LC record available at https://lccn.loc.gov/2022002038
LC ebook record available at https://lccn.loc.gov/2022002039

31 30 29 28 27 26 25 24 23 22   1 2 3 4 5 6 7 8 9 10 11 12

For those on the journey to educational justice and freedom work.

Cultivating Joyful Learning Spaces for BLACK GIRLS

1

The Framework: Schools as Locations for Healing

Teach me about what teaches you.
   —Malidoma Patrice Somé, *The Healing Wisdom of Africa*

Educators are purveyors of information that is transferred via pedagogy intended to reach a cross section of culturally and linguistically diverse students. They are also often first responders to students in crisis, which invites them to do more than simply convey information but rather to embrace the full child in holistic learning about not only subject matter but also who they are and what they contribute to their communities.

   In my book *Pushout: The Criminalization of Black Girls in Schools,* I describe how historical legacies of oppression and hyperpunitive, contemporary frameworks for safety in schools can foster learning conditions that weave schools into the tapestry of harm in Black girls' lives. From this discussion, and other studies examining the differential treatment of Black girls in schools, researchers have mapped the racialized gender bias that denies them access to instruction, unveiled differential enforcement of dress code policies that affect whether girls are allowed to attend school, and explored other surveillance and use-of-force measures that threaten Black girls' physical safety in schools. These policies, practices, conditions, and prevailing ideas about Black girlhood are what I have referred to as "school-to-confinement pathways,"[1] and they often justify educators' deep inquiry into combating pushout as an essential professional inquiry, as well as a moral and educational imperative.

School-to-Confinement Pathways

COVID-19 has dramatically altered the landscape of educational practices, expanding the United States' capacity for remote instruction. However, girls and femmes—young people who identify their gender along a continuum or as nonbinary and express in a traditionally feminine manner—who identify as Black, Indigenous, Latina, Asian, Pacific Islander, Arab, or other people of color have faced "difficulties adjusting to changes in the educational process, including inequitable access to reliable technology for distance learning, teacher support to address learning challenges, and reduced access to critical social and health services and supports normally provided within school settings."[2]

Even in these conditions, Black girls remain the only group of girls who are disproportionately overrepresented across the spectrum of discipline at every educational level. (According to a recent study by the Georgetown Law Center on Poverty and Inequality, the racial disparity in discipline is greater among girls than among boys.[3]) Compared with white girls, Black girls were more than 5 times more at risk of transfer for disciplinary reasons, approximately 4 times more likely to face expulsion, and 3.6 times more likely to be arrested on campus.[4] Although an increasing number of schools are developing alternative practices designed to divert students from exclusionary discipline, racial disparities persist among those who remain along the pathways to confinement. Stated simply, even though fewer students may experience exclusionary discipline, those who do are disproportionately Black.

School-to-confinement pathways for Black girls and femmes include unnecessary exclusionary discipline, which places them at risk of participation in underground economies, exacerbated trauma, and subsequent increases in their likelihood of future contact with the juvenile court and criminal legal systems. These pathways also include the citations and activities that occur at school and render Black girls vulnerable to increased surveillance and criminalization on campus. School dress codes and other codes of conduct that are written without the participation and coauthorship of girls, femmes, and their families often contribute to the adultification of Black girls and to school avoidance—both of which affect access to instruction and learning outcomes.[5] Adultification is also a form of dehumanization, as it strips Black girls of the ability to engage in their own experiences as a child or developing adolescent. It can also lead to adults being less patient with them when they make mistakes and to harsher punishments because they are believed to "know better" or to have a greater command of their expressions and behaviors than they may actually have, given their chronological age. In short, adultification obscures Black girlhood and renders it vulnerable to erasure, even in learning spaces that are supposed to protect and nurture developing adolescence.

The history of biased education codes and violent restrictions to learning in the Black community is unfortunately embedded in the structural and policy design of schools that educate Black girls and their peers. Such history triggers recollections of traumas when Black families are invited onto school campuses without recognition of how architecture and political infrastructure bare dehumanizing past practices that extend to both curricular and extracurricular involvement. Classrooms are institutional in design, often cold and uninviting. In some areas, schools are designed similarly to carceral facilities, where students may only congregate in areas that allow for elevated surveillance and monitoring, which is often not conducive to community building and play. To engage Black girls in developing their academic achievement, it is important for educators to recognize that it is not enough that a school be labeled as a "safe place." Educators must also uplift the epistemological considerations—such as the pedagogical practices that affirm the whole child and their language(s) and identities of origin—that make "safety" possible in learning.

Healing as a Prerequisite for Learning

Research finds that the overarching strategy for reducing the criminalization of Black girls involves developing a robust learning environment that prioritizes safety as it is defined by the girls most harmed by existing structures of oppression. From my work and discussions with Black girls, I have come to understand that schools need to be engaged as locations for *healing* so that they can be locations for *learning*. Healing facilitates safety. Safety facilitates joy. When students feel safe, their brain is more receptive to learning new material, as well as processing and developing ideas. When students feel unsafe, their brains are focused on protection from perceived threat or harm. In this mental state, it's hard to focus and make informed decisions. We can create schools that foster this level of healing work by doing the following:

- Developing a robust alternative to punitive, exclusionary discipline. This goal is accomplished by designing mechanisms to respond to trauma and pull students in closer when they are in crisis, rather than push them away. We also accomplish this goal by facilitating healing from trauma in schools such that they avoid becoming what I describe as "maladaptive classrooms" or "those punitive learning environments that have emerged in response to the prevailing racialized gender bias that disproportionately criminalizes Black and Brown girls."[6]

- Mapping the margins for our most vulnerable students to better recognize how students' multiple identities intersect to inform their relationships with school policies and practices and the resulting effects. This refers to Kimberlé Crenshaw's work on intersectionality, which invites a deeper exploration (using quantitative and qualitative methods) of the lived experiences of those whose identities predispose them to historical and structural marginalization from systems that improve social and economic conditions. An understanding of these intersecting identities (e.g., race, sex, ability, sexuality) helps educators develop remedies to the systemic harm generated by erasure or reliance on biased punitive discipline.

- Replacing law enforcement personnel with counselors, clinicians, and other youth-development specialists who can effectively facilitate healing activities that respond to dysregulation among students with regard to relationships and community and that have been determined as "central to restoring well-being."[7]

- Building curricula and other school-based structures that do not "teach to the oppression," a phrase that I use to describe how educators teach material that only presents or discusses the experience of a historically marginalized group (i.e., Black Americans, Indigenous/Native Americans) through a lens of oppression. For example, as I discuss in *Sing a Rhythm, Dance a Blues*, if students learn about Black Americans *only* through the lens of slavery and the modern civil rights movement, they are likely to understand the Black American experience only through that lens. However, if curricula and learning activities integrate the experiences of the diverse communities that compose this nation, then a richer collective liberation narrative emerges for our students. This is the narrative that allows students whose communities have been marginalized to feel seen and thus important. That is how we bring students in closer to their learning experience.

- Designing the school day (pacing and scheduling) to provide opportunities for pause, regulation, processing of learning, and social-emotional development.

- Designing the curriculum to affirm and engage Black girls and other students across racial, ethnic, and gender identities in the learning and to acknowledge the multiple ways that Black girls and other girls of color express their knowledge.

- Developing a school environment designed to secure the physical, emotional, and intellectual safety of culturally and linguistically diverse students (e.g., through use of affinity spaces, counselors, volunteers, relationships, empathetic responses to student misbehavior, yoga, mindfulness, restorative approaches).[8]

However, despite an abundance of evidence that these strategies are effective in reducing school pushout, unnecessarily punitive responses to student misbehavior remain a concern. This reality is partially a function of the rigidity and racially biased manner in which schools are applying their understanding of "effective" or "best" practices. It's time to extend epistemology—our practice of how knowledge is understood, acquired, and exchanged—and explore ways of developing pedagogical practices that honor the complexity of "knowing" and that invite us to cocreate new educational landscapes with and for girls of color, particularly Black girls.

Expanding the Nature of Knowing

In my book *Sing a Rhythm, Dance a Blues: Education for the Liberation of Black and Brown Girls,* I invite schools to understand how the application of best practices must be an ongoing process, a cyclical engagement, that requires us to bring our whole selves to the inquiry of education. Bridging the research-to-practice gap becomes more rigorous when educators invite into their practice the participatory elements that reflect what action research theorist John Heron, an architect of cooperative inquiry,[9] refers to as the *multiple ways of knowing.* Heron's engagement in and development of participatory research methods helped to demonstrate how understandings that are experiential (i.e., lived experiences of the affected populations), presentational (storytelling, art, etc.), propositional (quantitative data, etc.), and practical (applied) can inform the process of knowing.[10] A community of scholar advocates has applied this method to more deeply explore how to counter school pushout for Black girls and their subsequent criminalization.[11]

In addition to Heron's ways of knowing, intuition and memory—"the natural state of an awakened consciousness"[12] that is thematically represented among the African Diaspora as an "oral tradition" including "myths, philosophy, liturgies, songs, and sayings"—also figure prominently in the development of an approach to inquire about the lives of people of African descent. This African American tradition includes cyclical rhythms and nonlinear characterizations of time and logic,[13] which provide opportunities to move beyond inflexible interpretations of data toward new ways of bringing people safely into learning communities. Scholars examining how Black girls achieve have explored how Black girl literacies—expressed through verbal and nonverbal cues—have shaped their interpretation of and interactions with institutions, social constructs, and agents of various systems in the public domain.[14] These ways of knowing call us into a more intentional consideration of how to combat the complex social problems of racialized gender bias in education—and in particular, the administration and enforcement of school discipline. They also open up the possibility for a more expansive inquiry about how educators cultivate learning spaces that are committed to liberated learning.[15]

Confronting the Role of Power

Extending epistemology in the effort to develop schools as locations for healing will also elevate a conversation about *power*. Martin Luther King Jr. stated that "power without love is reckless and abusive . . . justice is power correcting everything that stands against love."[16] Fundamentally, raising questions about power helps us understand how sacred experience and theory could enhance the possibility of relationships that guide us toward recognizing the richness of an authentic, participatory experience, where we appreciate and love young learners enough to *learn with and from them,* rather than attempt to "treat" or "control" them. This possibility leads to a critical question of pedagogical practice: How will we use our power?

Our current emphasis, which I have argued is deeply problematic, is primarily about control—and it is exacerbating harm. For example, in January 2021, a 16-year-old girl in Florida was body-slammed by a police officer on campus after a fight broke out.[17] In a video that went viral, the officer is shown lifting the girl and slamming her body to the concrete, immediately handcuffing her as she lay unconscious on the ground. The incident joined a growing collection of occurrences involving Black girls and their interaction with school-based law enforcement officers, inviting a more rigorous interrogation of how Black girls experience school discipline.

But these incidents are more than problematic or tragic. What do incidents like this teach us? What do they reveal? What ideas and structures produce this harm? What is the impact of this harm on learning? What structures and responses could mitigate and eliminate this harm? How do these incidents reflect racialized gender bias in schools? These are some of the questions that educators and educational policymakers should be asking in the pursuit of cultivating safe learning spaces for Black girls—and all other students.

These are guiding questions, not rhetorical ones, in the effort to end school pushout. It is insufficient to merely explore Positive Behavioral Interventions and Supports (PBIS), restorative practices, social-emotional learning, or other interventions without a racial and gender analysis. The next iteration of this work—and the primary utility of this book—is to inspire educators to become immersed in interrupting school-to-confinement pathways for Black girls. This is necessary work.

Racial disparities among pushout-related incidents—both the egregious and the more routine (e.g., differential enforcement of school dress codes)—reveal how schools perceive and respond to Black bodies in schools. The responses to acts of student dysregulation also teach us about how our educational systems operate today as part of the tapestry of harm in Black girls' lives. They challenge us to consider why we have allowed our educational systems' responses to student behavior to continue in misalignment with the research-based best practices associated with responding to student misbehavior, which emphasize empathy, de-escalation of the sensitivity to threat, mindful breathing, and opportunities to restore and repair emotional safety and relationships. These strategies, and others that I have outlined in *Sing a Rhythm, Dance a Blues*, do not require police interventions.[18]

Looking Beyond *Who* to *What* Teaches Us

I opened this chapter with a quote from Malidoma Somé about teaching. Somé is a West African philosopher, healer, and educator who has invited deeply rigorous reflections about the human experience. His books about sacred African traditions have elevated indigenous wisdom (i.e., ancestral traditions) and customs that should inform pedagogical orientations that are being developed for students of color, particularly Black children. When, in the quote, Somé asks about what teaches us, it is an invitation to consider *all* that teaches. Teachers are not always standing in front of or beside us. Extending our lens to *what* teaches helps us find connections between research and practice such that we develop a *praxis* for orchestrating learning conditions that respond to intersecting conditions of oppression. Exploring what art, experiences, stories, and other expressions of knowing have to teach us about making meaning of best practice is an open invitation to challenge the historical and contemporary interpretations of who should have access to data and how we make sense of it.

Who teaches you? *What* teaches you? The answers to these questions are foundational for a deeper activation of our multiple forms of knowing. They invite us to a world of exploration that frees us to construct future learning spaces for liberation and healing, particularly for those deepest in crisis.

What I have observed as a student, a researcher, an educator, and a parent is that one of the greatest teachers is the healing journey. Yes, the journey is the *teacher*, not just the path. As a teacher, the healing journey guides the process for reflection, for analysis, for truth, for forgiveness, and for reconciliation and accountability. This teacher has high expectations—she is rigorous and a very tough grader. Our performance is measured not by how well we perform on a single assessment but by how we routinely engage with others, how we understand ourselves as individuals and in relation to other people, and how we extend opportunities for others to join our journey.

I would argue that education is ultimately a foundational element of the ability of the United States to prepare to meet its aspirational goal of being a "leader of the free world." But until our learning is liberated, the nation will remain enslaved to antiquated ideologies and behaviors that undermine the possibility of justice. Freedom is about the ability to move without restriction. To facilitate this degree of fluidity and promise, those who facilitate learning have to possess the skills to orchestrate well-being and healing in order to create conditions in the classroom that are conducive to learning.

What This Book Offers: Discussions to Inspire and Learn From

This book is written as a complement to my other two previously mentioned books on this subject: *Pushout: The Criminalization of Black Girls in Schools* and *Sing a Rhythm, Dance a Blues: Education for the Liberation of Black and Brown Girls*. Together, these previous texts define pushout and discuss the overarching contexts schools may engage to end harmful practices that facilitate the disproportionate criminalization of Black girls in schools. That conversation is for everyone.

The discussions in this book are specifically for those who create conditions for educational systems in the United States. They offer educators ideas about developing school communities that engage in an appreciative inquiry toward generating learning environments that support Black girls' excellence and academic achievement. That inquiry is the healing journey; that is the teacher. For this book, I have anchored a series of in-depth discussions—interviews and a virtual roundtable— with three educators: Venus Evans-Winters, Janice Johnson Dias, and Kakenya Ntaiya. They have uniquely relevant experience with building learning spaces that center this unequivocal, positive question about how schools can cultivate Black girls' excellence.

Venus Evans-Winters has a doctorate in education and a master's degree in social work from the University of Illinois at

Urbana-Champaign. She is a practicing clinical psychologist and scholar who has authored several books and articles on educating Black girls. Known as "Dr. V" among her students, clients, and advocates in the field, she has been called the "hip hop therapist." Evans-Winters is a former professor of education at Illinois State University in the College of Education with faculty affiliation in Women and Gender Studies, African American Studies, and Ethnic Studies. She is also the founder of Planet Venus and creator of the Write Like a Scholar program. She researches and teaches in the areas of social and cultural foundations of education, Black feminist thought, critical race theory, educational policy, and qualitative inquiry. With years of experience as a psychotherapist and a certified clinical trauma professional, Evans-Winters has embraced resilience-building practices throughout her work. She is also a licensed school social worker and youth advocate with experience in South Africa and West Africa, and she has participated in critical-pedagogy institutes (based on the work of Paulo Freire) across Europe. She is the author of several books, including *Teaching Black Girls: Resiliency in Urban Classrooms* and *Black Feminism in Education: Black Women Speak Back, Up, and Out*, and the coeditor with Bettina Love of *A Boss Chick's Guide to Mindfulness Meditation*.

Janice Johnson Dias, who earned a doctorate and a master's degree in sociology from Temple University, is a sociologist who has developed and administered programming for Black girls for more than two decades. Originally from Jamaica, Johnson Dias has been a high school English teacher and a teaching assistant, and she now holds a tenured faculty position at the City University of New York, John Jay College of Criminal Justice. She conceptualized and leads the GrassROOTS Community Foundation (GCF), where she heads a team that trains girls to be changemakers by showing them how to use their frustrations to solve social issues. In her work with local governments, she focuses on translating social science research into policy. Her work with corporations centers on identifying ways in which unrecognized privileges organize the workplace, pinpoints how racism and sexism structure the execution of work, and offers strategies on how to restructure for equity.

She has described herself as being from a "family of women who organize around things that have to do with women." Her book, *Parent Like It Matters: How to Raise Joyful, Change-Making Girls*, explores the lessons from her journey as a mother, daughter, and community leader in service to Black girls.

Both of these educators have tackled the questions at the core of this book in pursuing the orchestration of learning environments that are anchored in resilience and committed to the appreciative practice of supporting Black girl excellence. Through my conversations with them, I explore the notion that in the educational universe we create with and for Black girls, the primary epistemology for the scholar-practitioner should be rooted in participatory exchange. Because the knowledge is distributed, the methodology associated with how we build space for the development of new futures must also be participatory. To inspire the innovation that we seek from educators in order to cultivate joyful learning spaces, we must root our understanding in the ancestral and cultural traditions that call this purpose into being. As Lisa Delpit has stated, "People of color are, in general, skeptical of research as a determiner of our fates."[19] So for this work, I use the primary oral tradition to discover how schools may center Black girl excellence as they strive to become locations for healing in order to be locations for learning.

Also featured in this book is Kakenya Ntaiya. After earning a doctorate in education from the University of Pittsburgh, she returned to Kenya, where she founded and became the president of the Kakenya Center for Excellence, a primary boarding school for girls in the Maasai village of Enoosaen, and became a chief architect of educational opportunity for girls in her region of East Africa. Ntaiya founded Kakenya's Dream, an international nonprofit organization, to educate girls; end harmful traditional practices, including female genital mutilation and child marriage; and uplift her community. In 2009, the Kakenya Center for Excellence boarding school opened its doors, serving 30 students. Today she reaches thousands of young girls and community members each year through three holistic and girl-centered programs that she pioneered at Kakenya's Dream. Her work is transformative and inspirational—and worthy of our study as we seek to support liberated educational journeys for Black girls in the United States.

I invite educators, school leaders, educational policy developers, and curriculum designers reading this book to "listen" to our discussions about what schools should consider when starting this work to cultivate "righteous" schools for Black girls. I invite readers to process, with the four of us, our notes on what it means to orchestrate a joyful space for Black girls in schools and to engage communities as co-constructors of safety. Ultimately, I invite readers to ignite their radical and artistic imaginations to create a new vision—a new script, a new cadence and tone—for the learning spaces in which Black girls are being educated. The adultification and criminalization that Black girls experience, which facilitate and result in their school pushout, are not inevitable. We can create just and liberated learning environments for everyone if we set our intentions to do so. This book will be most useful to those who accept these invitations.

2

Getting Started: Key Considerations for School Leadership

Education is the most powerful weapon which you can use to change the world.

—Nelson Mandela

To be locations for healing, schools must reconcile the ways in which they facilitate harm. For educators and school leaders to be facilitators of healing, they must see themselves not as passive elements of the culture, just "getting through" an otherwise overwhelming environment. The same is true for curriculum design specialists, educational policymakers, and professional development leaders. They must all embrace and enthusiastically accept their own leadership on this issue and seek to confront the ways that they can map, analyze, and respond to the school culture they build with and for students. Getting started with this process also means being aware of key considerations associated with facilitating school as a location for healing for Black girls. This includes asking questions such as these:

- Why is it important for schools in general, and this school in particular, to address racial disparities in school discipline and other practices that we know can (intentionally or unintentionally) harm Black girls' educational outcomes?

- What is the level of readiness among school personnel—faculty, staff, contractors, and volunteers—to address this issue? How do we know this, or how do we gather the information we need to know this?
- Who needs to be a part of the conversations about the plight of Black girls in this school? Is there an existing relationship between the school and key stakeholders from the community (including a representative sample of Black girls themselves) served by this institution?

Venus Evans-Winters, Janice Johnson Dias, and I talked about these and other key considerations as schools launch a reconciliatory process toward the goal of establishing schools as disruptors of pushout. Here is our conversation.

MONIQUE

I invited us here to have a conversation about Black girls in schools because we are often perceived as the "exceptional" ones, even though we're perfectly representative of what's possible for all Black girls. We are perceived as the ones who were able to negotiate a system that has not been designed for us. I come to all of this work—my teaching work, my advocacy work, my research, my life—with who I am. I come as a professional, but also as a survivor of multiple structures of oppression.

Venus, that was one of the things that I remember from seeing you talk early on. I was like, I *get* her, I *know* her, and I want to have conversations with her, because we come from different places but the same community. And, you know, Janice, there is this way that people see you engage with your daughter that is also familiar to me. People see us as intellectual mothers who know how to grow young women who speak their truths and engage in solution building. And that's true! But the girls we're in community with, whether we physically birthed them or not, are just girls who are working through a whole lot of other things. They're working through stuff. Our young people are human.

So, I really want to engage you all in this conversation, because we're often asked to either lead professional development with teachers, or we're asked to give lectures to folks about how we cultivate educational spaces for Black girls. In many ways, people treat us as Black girl whisperers, right? [Laughs] But that's something that I have rejected. I think that it's really important not to mystify what it is that we're actually doing when we are supporting Black girls, and to really think about what goes into building a system that doesn't intentionally cause harm in their lives, that is so ambivalent to the structures of oppression that they're negotiating, or that doesn't do anything to combat that oppression either. So let's start there.

JANICE

That second point is the one that stays with me all the time. What happens when a Black girl manages to be successful in an unjust system? It often sends this message that there's nothing wrong with the *system* because *she* made it. That, to me, is one of the many ways in which the system reifies itself and justifies behaving in the most unjust, inequitable ways. It's like, *Oh, well, look at those three Black girls! I mean,* they *got accepted to Harvard;* they *got accepted to that prestigious school. There's nothing wrong for the rest of these kids.* They think, if they just worked as hard as those three did, they'd be fine, right? So Black girls' resistance and survival is seen as a sign that the system is working fine. And that is infuriating to me. It is the place where this notion of exceptionalism is fostered. They themselves do not recognize that even though they've endured, they have survived, and even if they've achieved by some material measures—that doesn't mean that what they experienced wasn't, in fact, harmful. It is more and more difficult, I think, in this particular social environment, to actually teach girls to see systems of inequity, especially high-achieving girls who have high levels of competency, because their singular focus is on their own survivorship.

I don't want to fault them for that, but I do want more attention to be paid to the fact that minimal success through an unjust, unfair, violent system is not what we want. We do not need to be pushing an F-150 up a hill. We need a system that makes it normative, easy, just for *all* children to move through. We need a system that pays attention to the fact that it has built in it a lot of anti-girl, anti–Black girl, anti-Black in general, unjust things, and successful kids really have to be called to task to see it and to try to do what they can—if their resources allow—in revamping it. People do not often listen to the kids who are failing. And we don't have a model like that currently. I need to see that model.

VENUS

You know, I think the ideas around exceptionalism and this model of Black girlhood is dangerous. Janice, you've said that you come from a family where the women are just ordinary people—that they wouldn't stand out on the street. And that's dynamic.

More recently, I've started to see all of these "Black exceptionality" stories in social media. For Black girls, they'd layer it. When sharing a Black girl's story, she has to be everything! She has to compose. She has to be the best at ballet. She must have a perfect SAT . . . a perfect ACT score. She had 100 acceptance letters and scholarships. . . . And I'm like, when did she *play*? And I mean, Black women are the ones who are spreading the news, right? They're the ones sharing these stories. And, of course, what do they do? They tag me in these stories, so then I choose whether to support the story or speak out against it for its exceptionalism! It's not to pathologize the kid who was able to achieve all of that or what it took for their families to help them achieve that; but we have no accountability system put in place for the other hundreds of thousands of Black girls who don't have the opportunity to become that, to achieve, or to thrive in a healthy environment. So that's the challenge with exceptionalism and all the "magic" and the "rocking." It's like, when do we get to be human? And when do Black girls get to have their humanness protected?

JANICE

I think that this issue of humanity is not trivial—especially in terms of errors and the ability to make fault and recover. That seems to be totally absent from the narrative of all Black girls, but particularly absent from high-achieving Black girls. I've marshaled an in-home campaign about this. I just want to say this, because I have a high-achieving Black girl who I really need to make mistakes. And I need it before she leaves my house. She does not understand why that's important, so I've been going on 10 months of this campaign about the reduction of humanity and the need to sometimes mess up, to let go, to be fragile, to be vulnerable. And I mean it from the emotional state—from the "bad friend" choices to all of it. Without it, there's a reduction of Black humanity.

When I talk, I tell people that they've relegated Black girls and Black women to superhuman or inhuman—both of which are *not* human. And you have to fight for humanity and fight to have a range of emotions, a range of experiences. And if you don't do that fight, people will relegate you to one of these boxes. They will say, *Oh my God, you're just above everything else!* Or, *Oh my God, you don't even rise to anything.* That is consistent. And it's consistent for Black girls in a particular form very early. It's easy to kind of just drink that, to take that in, and have that be the thing you're sipping on every day. And so trying to get the girl herself and the system itself to see how it creates these things—that you either have to be superhuman or you're inhuman—that is a charge. And it is a part of the kind of mantle I've taken up because we designed a program called "Branches" for high school girls in Newark, New Jersey.

In Newark, 27 percent of the people live below the poverty line.[1] The high school we work in is in a particularly poor neighborhood, and it's a beautiful school. It's a community school, so it's open 24 hours a day. When I went to recruit for the program, they all wanted to send me their "amazing" Black girls, and our liaison there had to intervene.

I was like, *Yo, I don't want your all-dolled-up girls, right? I want girls across the gamut.* And she was like, *You want these bad-ass kids?* And I said, *Yes, I do. I do want these bad-ass kids.* And she was like, *You're always so good with them bad-ass kids.* I said, *Well, you know, I was a kid who didn't get caught.*

I'm happy I didn't get caught; I really am. But people mistake not getting caught with having never done it, right? And again, I had resources to help me not get caught. We underestimate the genius of the girls when we're only looking in one little spot in the honors classes or in the AP classes.

So we had that program at that school for four years and got a whole host of girls that people would otherwise think couldn't do anything. But when they organized the two conferences that we had there, people were like, *She is on the organizing committee?* And I'm like, *Yeah, she's the one who's going to be the moderator!* And, you know, it gives girls an opportunity to be seen in other ways than just the ways that they're being seen in the classroom or the ways their families are seen, or the way they're seen with whoever they are touching or feeling on. And for me, I just think that that's wickedly important because when we do prize specific things like looks, etc., we lose the multidimensional ways in which Black girls are. And those multidimensional ways are what I call humanity. It is what I am. I'm really trying to push for people to see that, yes, there are some times we're magic, some times we're ornery, and both are right, depending on the circumstance.

MONIQUE

Well, part of how I have been framing this adultification issue that Black girls experience in schools is that it is a form of dehumanization. There are many things that schools do to facilitate adultification of Black girls, and what we haven't spent as much time on are the things that schools need to have in place to disrupt that. I think each of us has addressed core components of it in terms of building out spaces that are resilient or that recognize resilience among Black girls, and understanding that resistance is not necessarily a bad thing among Black girls. Then, also thinking about this role of joy and how it manifests in the learning space and among people who work with them.

I really want to address how schools could actively think through how they are going about *humanizing* our girls in a way that provides them this maximum opportunity to thrive. The school is likely not going to be able to do it all alone, and so who else needs to be in the mix? You have a program that goes into a school, so then you become a partner to the school. What do these partnerships need to look like? What does the institution need to have in place in order to receive these partnerships in a way that we know does the best service to our Black girls and other young people of color?

JANICE

I clearly have lots of thoughts on this because I've run programs in the schools for the past decade. Schools have to invest in the people. And I'm just really super clear that a part of the reason why schools don't know how to partner with kids and communities is that they just don't think of themselves as being in *partnership*. The word *partner* suggests input and collaboration from multiple entities, and schools just don't organize themselves that way. Furthermore, schools put a lot of people in front of kids who are suffering in their own lives. And people who are suffering are not going to be facilitators of joy or of learning, or of a whole host of things.

When I was working with a school in Greensboro, I had to interview every person who was interested in running the program. We paid a good fee, and many people wanted to participate; and then hearing that they couldn't, some were unsure about why they couldn't. We had some objective measures. One of the objective measures was that they needed to live in the neighborhood for at least the past five years—the ones that the girls we were serving lived in. That was really critical to me. The other was that they needed to define the word *racism*. That was also critical. And the third was to describe for us what they thought the definition of *excellence* was, as a measure. Those were our three interview questions outside of having their résumé. What we found from those answers is that for the excellence question and the racism question, people define them as individual matters. And if they had only individualism in the response, then they weren't eligible to work with our programs.

We knew we were going to get a lot of white folks who were going to apply, and we didn't want to push out white folks. We just really wanted to make sure that the white folks that we worked with understood that they would be working with Black girls. And we also needed them to recognize that while we're skill-developing the girls and trying to get them to be healthy, it's because we want them to then push back on a *system*. And if they don't have a systems framework, then they're going to end up only being like, *I helped this little girl learn how to run a 5K race,* and not understand why that's related to systemic change.

MONIQUE

Without a systems analysis, if that Black girl begins to use some of those organizing skills to transform the system, she could be vulnerable to a heightened degree of discipline.

JANICE

Yes. So the first answer is, we have to make real investments in the girls. The second is, I think schools are not treated as the intersection of family, community, and government. I think that schools have to figure out how to engage family, and particularly family as it relates to work, and community as it relates to the presence of violence—at this point, overt violence. The walk to school, the bus stop, the routes. All of those things. And government—it's the legislative rules. And so those entities all need to be asked questions like, *Who are the representatives of these entities? Do they understand this as a web?* I think if schools did that, they would make some small step forward. I'm just so concerned about the way that schools are currently organized. We've got to imagine a different construction of schools.

MONIQUE

That's been the work. I totally agree. We've got to reimagine the function of schools, but also what they look like, what pedagogical approaches we're using, and how our biases are informing what we teach. The whole thing. If you think about what schools look like, and how they are built, and how we prepare educators to go into these spaces—and then on top of that, this layer of how we now have our young people walking down the halls with hands behind their back in lines like they are in the juvenile detention center. What are we doing? There's a lot of stuff happening to prime our young people for something else, for criminalization, rather than excellence and community. I agree with you on this point about the schools needing to be reconfigured as a place where this collective learning and collective engagement occur. This is where there must be an intentional disruption. Also, schools should be aesthetically pleasing. They should be beautiful.

JANICE

Even the best and most attractive schools, they're just not *beautiful*. I feel like I selected my kid's preschool because it was so cute, OK? It was cute! Inside the classroom was a cute little bathroom. The chairs were cute. At pickup, I'd be like, *I just want to sit in your classroom because it's so cute*. It had different things that you could touch. It was inviting! Invitation like that goes away as soon as they start to move through the educational system. And I'm like, *This is not fun.*

My husband is a good American, and he was like, *Well, y'all sat outside* [at a school in Jamaica]. And I was like, *Yeah, imagine how much more interesting that is than sitting in four walls all the time!*

The school scheduling is crazy, and it's just so uninteresting. And this is where private schools end up winning, because they have the autonomy to make decisions like taking class outside. And they're structurally organized in a more interesting way because they have opulence at their fingertips. I want places where kids can congregate and learn from brilliant people and engage and tackle and develop their thinking and writing.

VENUS

Some of the *people* aren't inviting. I mean, we opened up this meeting by talking about lipsticks and hair—but these are the things that are taken for granted. As a people, whether we're talking about the civil rights movement; whether we're talking about schools being highly successful, or segregated schools in the 1950s and the '60s; whether we're talking about the Nation of Islam, Jesse Jackson, or Al Sharpton . . . there's an aesthetic that Black people really appreciate. The people who we are expecting to lead our children need to know this.

I remember there was one time I was at my daughter's high school basketball game, and there was this teacher who was overseeing the entrance. She actually had her legs propped up with her feet on the table where you pay for the tickets. She was young, white, and wearing these black leggings and a black sweater. And I remember saying to her, *Oh, you're really relaxed, aren't you?* You know, Black-speak, where the listener is required to read in between the lines. And the Black guy sitting next to her—he knew exactly what I was saying—looked me in the eyes and gently nodded to cosign on my observation (and message).

She put her legs down and said, "Oh, I thought we were at a basketball game."

Well, you're also a teacher who is a role model all the time, even at a basketball game! This is just an example of how so many teachers convey a message that they don't care about us. It signals that many young white teachers think that we have no standards or ethics of care. You're a teacher! You're wearing your teacher's badge! I don't care if it's a game or not. And this is not about the politics of respectability. It's about what you are asking of the students. Will they be able to see you and respect you as a potential leader in their school?

And there was one time when my son was little and in elementary school, and a preservice teacher was co-teaching. It was a kindergarten or 1st grade classroom. The teacher had on leggings and flip-flops. . . . We called them "shower shoes" at the time, because we used to wear them literally in the shower at college so we wouldn't get our feet dirty. Her T-shirt was up to here [gestures to the area just above her belly button].

I remember telling the principal, who happened to be a student of mine at the time and who was learning about culturally responsive leadership, about my concerns.

I said, "We have a problem. We know that this young woman is coming from an affluent, private liberal arts university. She's coming into this predominantly poor school district, and she's presenting herself this way in front of mothers and fathers, and even the children, because she doesn't believe that we have standards of care and behavior."

How she showed up to the classroom tells us that she has no expectations for herself as a leader in that classroom, and that's because she thinks that we have no standards for our children and classroom teachers. To be clear, I'm not saying that the kindergarten teacher who's going to be teaching PE class needs to be dressed in a suit, but I am saying that there's an aesthetic to Blackness that I don't think educators should take for granted. The physical environment counts, and how you show up counts!

JANICE

I want to expand on that idea, because I think that this notion of how people show up sends a message that you matter. I think it's underdiscussed, because it's usually framed as a respectability conversation. I think all of us see that that has real limits, even though it is a structural risk response, and I don't think it actually has been given enough public inquiry, because it's usually masked in conversations about Black boys and the pant/necktie game. It has not really demonstrated to people that, really from the 1920s to 1960s, a failure to present correctly has cost Black people. For example, Black women lost their children to child welfare because they weren't dressed appropriately. So, like, I think the popular culture doesn't understand that this attention to clothing is a response to a structural assault on our children, that reads of our socioeconomic status. Black folks read the way white folks dress in front of us as a way of categorizing whether or not they care about us. I think that's unknown, and I think that, given that Black folks are a significant population of public school students and white teachers and administrators are the dominant people in front of them, that's a gift that we could give to them. Present yourself to the children, and to their caregivers, as if you care. Tell us whether or not you think there is value. It actually invokes the message: You matter. Those are the kinds of things I think of when we think about racial competency.

MONIQUE

Our presentation matters, and it's always mattered. It's mattered on Sunday morning, you know, more than any other day. It mattered on Saturday night. It doesn't always translate, and I think it also doesn't always translate in the way we want it to translate. Because when we invite conversations about how people "should" dress in the schools, it's often used as a tool for punishment. Black students are punished when they show up any old kind of way, and they're especially punished if it can, in any way, be read as "provocative." And so, I think that what we've got to do, particularly around increasing the school's capacity to have meaningful conversations about competency, is to be able to read and recognize what is appropriate for us outside of the lens of the middle class, faith-based norm you may hold. Really, it's about how you present in a way that demonstrates to other people that they matter.

It actually leads me to think about, I guess, some of the epistemological considerations that you, Venus, have been elevating about how schools and educators need to prepare to teach Black girls. You may not speak a word, but how you come, as well as your energy, whether you decide to comb your hair or not, all of that matters. And it feels superficial to a culture that has had the privilege of not having to present in a specific way to be received as human, or have their humanity argued on those terms. But it is absolutely something that matters to us. And I would argue it goes back to ancient knowings about values that are shared throughout the diaspora.

VENUS

I think this has something to do with who's valued, who's devalued, who's seen as valuable, and whose values are proliferated through our school systems. I think the problem with some partnerships is just like that of many other things in our school systems: we still have a corporate model. We still have this idea that partnerships are something like collateral. They're commodified. So how can I *benefit* from your profits or your resources? And we're still thinking about it in a currency kind of way. We need to shift from this idea of corporate-like partnerships to *collaborations*. Collaborations. Collaboration looks more like we have a shared responsibility; we equally have something to lose or to gain from this relationship. Collaboration looks like bringing in grandmothers. Can a grandmother actually lead the reading circle? Can that older sister be the one who actually takes the kids back and forth to the playground? You know, incorporating the family, the community, and others in the school.

It's not a coincidence that we're talking about values and aesthetics. Research shows that students in schools, they're not necessarily going to follow just any teacher. I don't care how nice you are; there are certain dispositions and certain characteristics young people gravitate toward in a leader. And if we can figure that out in our collaborations, we'll move away from business models that dehumanize and commodify our children. Ontologically speaking, children are so sophisticated that they're picking up on people's spirits—no standards or standards? I think what's happening now is that we're in a culture where we are afraid to talk about standards, and that's because we've had these binaries. And it's like, *Am I Lil' Kim? Am I Nicki Minaj? Am I Cardi B, or am I Megan Thee Stallion? Or am I Kamala Harris? Am I Stacey Abrams? Am I Oprah Winfrey?* There's nothing in between where I can just be this ordinary person who is judged based on my humanity. I bring value to humanity. I have rights.

JANICE

I agree that the way the current system operates is a system that is most businesslike. It's transactional, and it is hierarchical. The thing that I think also happens is that the children *read* it as that [transactional] space. So the system operates that way, and I think that's a mistake. They read the institution as not caring about them and as being transactional with them. And so they engage in a relationship that is antilearning. This is not a healing space. And so I get it. You're here to make sure that you get paid.

And schools, I think, are not understanding that when they engage in a relationship that is so nonreciprocal, the authority is not just theirs. Children respond to the authority by co-opting whatever power they have. The power they have, they will utilize. They are governed by law, up until the time they're 16, to engage in this kind of relationship with them. It is the legislative law of the land. The kids know the rules too. They know that they're engaging in it, but I think schools operate like the kids don't know.

You want a *partnership*, but right now the school systems have the *power*. And you all are here to play your roles. But the power lies with us, and we are missing the fact that when you seek to oppress people, people will take their power—and they will take it in whatever way they can. So what we've seen in these outcomes, and in these internal experiences, is people fighting to have some agency over their lives. They simply cannot just give up their power to a system; they just won't do that. And if schools saw Black kids, especially Black girls, as human, they would recognize that. They're human. They want to matter.

MONIQUE

So much of how we structure partnerships is aligned with what you all have been saying around this transactional corporate structure losing sight of the kinds of relationships that need to be in place, and the kind of repair that needs to take place between schools and communities. Schools were part of a tapestry of harm in their lives for so long. If parents are afraid to step on campus, or parents don't want to step on campus because it triggers negative feelings because they've had a bad experience, then yes, it's always going to function in the community as a place where they don't want to have to go. If the only interaction remains contentious, like a competitive space or feeling, or if you have to look a certain way to belong in a conversation about the well-being of your child, or you have to have a certain vocabulary for the educator to take you seriously, then it's going to be a problem. It's going to be a big problem.

JANICE

When kids are young, and in preschool and kindergarten, there is the sense that it doesn't matter who you are: mom, dad, uncle, or grandma. Everybody can come and pick up the child, until around 3rd grade. Then there is this erosion in relationships. From 3rd grade on, there is the sense of like, *What's the teacher gonna say to me?* The power dynamic shifts, and then the known hostility becomes present, and caregivers start to be pushed out. They start to feel misaligned with what is happening. I try to get caregivers that I work with to recognize that what they're feeling is right. The system is doing that to them. Caregivers start to have an instinct, and it's the same kind of thing that happens with girls. You know when something's up, but you mostly think it's *you*.

I asked my friends to do a thing for me, because I spend a lot of time with my friendship groups talking about racism. I was like, *Look, check yourself. Did you sleep well last night?* And then I said, *Well, did you drink enough water today?* They're like, *I did, but I still have this headache.* And I was like, *You didn't have a lot of sodium?* They're like, *No.* And I was like, *Well, racism might be what's getting you. That might be the reason for the headache.*

Oftentimes what happens with individuals is that they think they're the problem. Once you have diagnosed that you're the problem, you're going to do a lot of "you" work. Once you start recognizing that it's the system that's trying to kill you, it's a different game.

Something happens right around 3rd grade and leading into middle school that intentionally functions to push community and family out. Schools start to prioritize these kinds of core business models, antigirl, anti-Blackness models. That's when Black girls' bodies are so heavily regulated. I'm finding in the urban schools that I've been working with, and even now in my daughter's suburban school, that Black girls are deemed as too provocative, too sexual. Their bodies are "too big." Racism is so funny, because it just morphs. Now it's, *She doesn't even dress like a girl.*

The system is always trying to find new ways of managing, controlling, and commoditizing Black girls' bodies through the heteronormative lens and a very specific, European framework.

MONIQUE

That's the policing of Black girls' bodies. We have to be in a space where we're clear that whatever policies are being developed need to not facilitate oppression of any kind. And these policies need to explicitly say that; and teachers, principals, and administrative staff need training and support around that.

VENUS

And their spaces have to portray that. I've walked into spaces that were forcibly desegregated and that are now predominantly Black. You walk into the school office and there's still a white principal, there's still a white administrative assistant who's answering the phone. The gate-keeper, the police officer, is also white. You look on the walls, and the school has been desegregated for at least 10–15 years, but they still got the white basketball team on the wall. They got all the white principals from the 1960s. You can see that all of their alumni, and their donors, they're all white. And it's all done intentionally. So you have that parent who is like, *I don't know why they're saying everybody belongs, that everybody's welcome.* The school has been desegregated for 50 years, and now it's predominantly Black, but you're still celebrating whiteness. You're saying whites are still in charge.

MONIQUE

You're saying, *Those were the "good old days."* That's what we see when we walk in. I'm so glad you brought that up, because that is part of the importance of recognizing multiple ways of knowing, which I'm hopeful [is the message] that educators take from our discussion. This is one of the areas where schools need to demonstrate that they are actively going to participate in dismantling these structures and representations of oppression. Photos are part of the structure, part of the landscape. These images that you put up of your "notable alumni" and your "beloved" alumni in public and private institutions often read as a celebration of exclusion, especially to Black students and other students of color who are walking through the halls. I've seen girls and boys go through these photos and start counting how many Black people they can find in these old pictures. I used to do that! You search through the photos, and suddenly it's like, *Oh, look! There's a Black person!* My daughter went to the same school that I went to in San Francisco, and one day, she was like, *Oh, Mom, we were looking at you today.* It was so easy to find me. [Laughs]

So it's the searching that our young people do for us that tells us that we are missing from the narrative of these schools. The normalcy of seeing yourself as always having been a part of something great, and knowing that you're still there, is a power play.

JANICE

I don't think schools even recognize this. I mean, this is the work of intentionality. The idea is that a school needs to articulate explicitly that its dress code is not going to be oppressive. What's so consistent about America, and particularly these anchor institutions, is that it just does not have enough investigation of itself. And so they go about their business. Schools will be like, *Well, I never thought about the pictures on the wall. We're so focused on girls, and children, trying to learn grammar.* They do not see that as a part of it. And so when they are told that, they're like, *Are you trying to suggest that we intentionally do not want to admit our Black students?* And that is one of the core functions of racism—the "never minding" of the fact that there are Black and Brown people in these spaces.

So administrators and teachers have to ask themselves, what are they *not* thinking of? Who are they *not* thinking about as they make the rules? [Professor, author, and TV/radio commentator] Melissa Harris-Perry says, "Well, who's missing here? Where's Keisha? Like, did you think about Keisha when you thought about constructing the design? Do you think she would feel validated in the space? Do you think the curriculum centers her? Do you think the space makes her feel warm and welcome?"

They default to what feels familiar to them, which sends this whole idea of legacy. They're like, *Well, we have a particular tradition and a particular right.* These are the anchor words: We have a *"tradition."* You see it with the statues in the United States—there's a particular "tradition." All of these institutions hold on to the past; then it becomes a cherished way of maintaining and polishing bigotry, racism, and institutional injustice. As faculty and administrators, these educators need to be aware of when they are doing this by asking themselves a set of core questions, such as *Who is missing in what? In the curriculum, the space, the lunch? Who's missing?*

MONIQUE

What is the impact of a decision, specifically on Black girls? Ask the question! Is this going to cause harm? What are we leading with when we implement this? Are we leading with love, or are we leading with fear? What about joy? Joy is such an essential part of learning.

These acts—the small ones and the large ones—are part of what makes learning a very nonjoyous experience for Black girls and Black boys. Our Black children are trying to learn in these spaces where they're in this constant state of having to be hyperaware of their difference, having to negotiate the white nostalgia, etc. Thinking about all these things can strip you of your joy—the joy of learning, your joy of being in school. You'll want to avoid it; you'll want to fight it; you'll want to cut it out. You'll just want to be combative, because you feel that you are in combat.

So when we think about this role of joy in creating *just* schools, what do you think needs to be in place?

VENUS

It's funny. I was just thinking of the song [by Maze, featuring Frankie Beverly] . . . "joy, and pain, sunshine and rain." That's what I was thinking. [Laughs] In Buddhist psychology, we do talk about these parallels.

You have joy, and you have pain in order to appreciate joy. Well, we're talking about Black joy, Black pain, and how we grapple with both simultaneously—what happens when love and rejection become tied to ideas of school success? School success at what cost?

I'm starting to see in my practice the long-term effects, the latent effects, of what's happening in our schools. When girls are told, *You gotta make it by any means necessary, even by giving up your own identity,* guess what happens to those girls? They're now experiencing depression and anxiety at high rates. Reports are coming in that Black women are reporting higher rates of loneliness. Loneliness is directly tied to cardiovascular diseases. The girls talk about self-care, and I ask, *What does self-care look like for you?* And they'll say, *Girl, I got my full set.* Whoa! Like [feminist poet and activist] Audre Lorde was a lesbian woman from the Caribbean who was battling cancer, racism, and homophobia while raising Black children. What she meant by personal care might be a little different than a full set of nails!

So we have to unpack how not to manage kids' emotions and ways to reteach adults how to allow children to be dynamic and fully human so that they won't become cyborgs—that they can have compassion, not just for others, but also for themselves.

MONIQUE

That's it for me. And that's why I've spent so much time on this criminalization and discipline conversation in schools. Our reaction to young people who are expressive of their emotions is failing us, for the sake of ease, for the sake of perpetuating the structures of violence that make it easier to criminalize whole communities.

There was a lack of rigor around some of the racist intents of scholars and practitioners in the 1980s and 1990s. What we got were a series of school policies that mirror this criminal legal system and stripped our schools of the capacity to really fully embrace young people who can express their learning across a range of emotions. And we watched it take place. Not all of us have a short memory! As the 1990s and early 2000s started to demonstrate for us that there were consequences associated with young people expressing joy, rage, fear, or frustration, we wanted to make sure they knew the ways of the system so they wouldn't get in trouble. We wanted them to at least make it through.

I remember having a conversation with one of my close friends about her son being placed in a Montessori school. As she was looking for the schools, she was like, *I think I'm going to go with Montessori.* She said, *I really loved it, but I have one problem.* And I was like, *What is it?* And she said, *It's that he is a tall Black child. He's a boy, and he's going to learn that he can call people by their first names and engage how they want to engage and move around the classroom and get up and walk around when he wants to. And then I'm going to take him out of this Montessori school, put him in another school, and he's going to get in trouble all the time.* And I remember being struck by her fear. I mean, she's an attorney, right? She's somebody who could see where this was headed. Other kids may have that freedom, but the sad belief is that our children are not going to have those same freedoms. Ultimately it was a conscious decision on her part to place him into a school that would teach him the ways of structure. For so many of our schools, the rhetoric—and consciousness—that is used for introductions reflects this debilitating idea: "This will be a *disciplined* environment, because Black and Latino children need *discipline.*"

All of these are ways that made me intentionally hyperaware of how this plays out in our community narratives. I wanted to show my daughters what free Black children look like. We would walk in different places and I'd be like, *You see that child?* And they'd be a child with unkempt hair playing. I was like, *That's a free Black child. And I want you to be free. And you will have hiccups in your life like we all do, but I need you to feel like you can experience freedom.*

I didn't have a free Black childhood. My mother was definitely "old school," so you could only be but so "free." [Laughs] I wanted it to be clear that freedom was possible, because that, to me, is also how we begin to disrupt these harmful narratives and practices about why—and how hard—we need to "whoop" our children. So, many of our schools are giving our children the proverbial whoopin' for being frustrated with systems that should make any person who's paying attention to it frustrated.

VENUS

Yeah, it is not just a whooping, because I want to be clear, we also have to grapple with the civic deaths of Black girls—in policies, in praxis. There are different forms of death. You have your corporal death where your body actually dies, and civil death where you can actually lose your civil rights as a citizen. There's also spiritual death, and that's where racist institutions are killing us softly. I'm concerned when I have girls who can't bounce back, and I'm concerned when I have adults who are in their late 20s, early 30s, and they're abusing alcohol. They're abusing their bodies, and a lot of it starts with schools. We haven't held schools accountable, because the lane for success is so narrow.

JANICE

My concern for educational institutions in the United States and the world at large is that there is a framework that says that life should be *more* pain than joy. And this framework is institutionalized in educational facilities. It says that this should not be fun. This should not feel good. If you're going to be successful, it should be laborious and hard— even obstructive. That is the framework that our children start to enter after 3rd grade.

But there's another framework—one that is fun to try to understand and learn. It's a framework that stays for white families, particularly white, middle-class families, throughout their entire experience. Learning is seen as enriching to human development, as central to your being. And then for others it's, *Well, for you, though, you need to really take this seriously, because you've got to get a job.* Or it's, *Not all of y'all are going to get into college.* The doublespeak gets institutionalized. So some kids are having joyful experiences, and others are having oppressive experiences. And those "others" are often Black girls.

They're stuck in this system. There are rules, and the rules are very clear. They say that as a Black girl, you need to operate under this kind of framework, and that framework is institutionalized, and then it is internalized. And that internalization people read as "attitudes." The system creates the context for oppression, and then it punishes the people who react to that context.

We need to structure a society where joyfulness has priority. We need to structure institutions where joyfulness and learning are in relationship with each other, not the reverse. Because currently it's structured that joyfulness is some offshoot that *may* happen for you in retirement, but for this portion of your life, especially if you are Black and especially if you're a Black girl, you should suffer. These are your suffering years. I just think it's a grave injustice to have these years be children's suffering years.

I think that this is also a part of Black girls' humanity that doesn't get talked about. People see their responses as not thoughtful, as not intellectually rigorous. They've thought about it, and they are deciding. That's the humanity they tried to erase from Black girls and from Black people—the fact that they were critically analyzing, choosing to respond, or negotiating. It doesn't matter that there may be errors in the calculus. We're not just bodies. We have agency, thought, and action—and your system has created this structure. And so we're trying to negotiate it. If we structure the school environment as a joyful place, it becomes about learning. And that is antioppressive. We can articulate that. We can normalize it, and we can codify it.

Takeaways for Your Practice

Joy is an essential part of learning. The foundations for creating joyful learning environments that also support Black girls' academic achievement require that we create conditions that allow them to feel safe and loved. This is repeated in this book and thus a foundational consideration for your practice. Safety is co-constructed through relationships—not simply by implementing a program or system of surveillance.

Authentic relationships and ongoing engagements to cultivate trust with one another allow for students and educators to bring themselves to the learning process with an open mind to dismantle biases that lead to judgment or reprimand. Many educational practices have the deleterious effect of interrupting the development of relationships, and thus, joyful learning experiences. Behavioral protocols that mimic carceral systems, pedagogical practices that only acknowledge Eurocentric values as valid, and other school-based learning activities may be leading to the undesired effect of alienating students who are culturally and linguistically diverse, such as Black girls. To advance toward more equitable conditions that provide a foundation for the ongoing work of revising policies and practices that render Black girls vulnerable to school pushout, schools must consider how they transform themselves into conduits for healing and transformation. This is not simple work, and it begins with an honest, intentional practice of self-examination.

Investigate Yourself and Your Institution

Commit to self-examination and reflection toward building an anti-racist, antisexist learning institution. Bettina Love writes in *We Want to Do More Than Survive* that we can move toward this goal through abolitionist teaching, which she describes as "the practice of working in solidarity with communities of color while drawing on the imagination, creativity, refusal, (re)membering, visionary thinking, healing, rebellious spirit, boldness, determination, and subversiveness of abolitionists to eradicate injustice in and outside schools."[2] Racism and racialized gender bias are exhausting and can be felt in many different ways. They are exacerbated by the corporate model that reduces the visibility and joy of Black girls and their families. This situation requires remedy.

Be Able to Define Racism and Develop a Complex Racial and Gender Analysis Using an Intersectional Frame

Intersectionality is a framework that understands how individuals' complex identities intersect to form unique vulnerabilities to institutions and structures in society. As more than just a recognition that these identities exist, intersectionality as a framework for developing a rigorous racial and gender analysis informs the development of perceptions and practices that map the margins and protect those most vulnerable to oppression.[3] This "mapping" involves data collection, as knowing your school's data—across a spectrum of decision-making points—is an important first step to being able to develop a robust racial and gender analysis with respect to school discipline trends and their contributing factors. However, collecting data with an eye toward who may be missing from the data, or whose experiences may be obscured by the way questions are asked and data collected, is essential.

Make Schools Inviting to Parents—and Students

Families should see and feel that their school believes they are a priority and that they are active participants in their learning community, not just a population to be corralled or "served." Partnerships and engagements with others cannot be structured as transactional if they are to be sustainable.

Recognize That Presentational Knowing Is an Important Part of Establishing a Climate of Respect with Black Families and Communities

Keep (but consider whether to display) your old photos of alumni—even if they harken back to a period of segregated opportunity; but have active discussions about how the school has been part of a narrative that either supports or rejects equal access to a high-quality education—and how it is working to remedy past harms. Strive to include other images that signal to the current student population that they are valued and centered in the school's current climate.

Build a Culture of Support for Black Girls That Recognizes How Each of Them Is Standing Boldly in Her Gifts

Instead of ignoring, undermining, or criminalizing their gifts, work with Black girls to celebrate and recognize that every girl—not just the ones who are performing at a high level at that moment—have the potential for leadership. For example, if a student is particularly loquacious, to the point of disruption, instead of removing her from the classroom, schedule time to speak with her privately. In that meeting, ask her why she is continually speaking out of turn. Chances are, she'll respond with some version of "I don't know," "Sometimes I get bored," or "I just think things are funny." Whatever her response, try not to internalize her experience, and instead, find a way to notice (aloud) that she is observant and still a valued part of the learning community. Then, find a way to honor what she needs to exercise her leadership—and observations—in a semi-structured way. Maybe offer her an opportunity to lead a "respondent corner," where she spends five minutes or so at the end of a lesson or class exploring what she thought was funny or deserving of comment. Acknowledging her gift as a spontaneous, observant student invites her to consider how she can bring those attributes to her learning experience, rather than be marginalized because of them.

Clearly this approach works best if the educator has an established relationship with the student, but you do not have to know the student well in order to lead the conversation with care. For *Pushout,* I spoke with girls who had been suspended about what they do during their time away from school. One in particular mentioned planning fights. At the end of her elaborate description of the process, I pointed out that she is an organizer. It was clearly the first time she'd considered her gift outside of a problematic context. Being an educator means leaning into the learning opportunity of every experience. Again, the question *What teaches you?* is not rhetorical. The actions that may be disruptive or distracting also teach us something about that student and her gifts. We can work with the student to unpack what those are and how they can be used as a tool for learning and growth.

Grieve the Harms of Institutional Bias

Each of the actions just described is preliminary and should be understood as an initial step toward reconciling the truth that although education is viewed by marginalized populations as a tool for liberation, educational institutions have historically been part of the tapestry of harm by reinforcing dangerous social norms and disproportionately priming Black children across the gender continuum for punishment and institutionalization. To move toward the development of educational institutions, practices, and pedagogies that are equitable and just, those who design, lead, and support these institutions must walk through the process of grieving the loss of status and privilege that many institutions have enjoyed to the detriment of its culturally and linguistically diverse students. Grieving the harms of institutional bias launches the process of truly repairing and transforming the relationship between schools and Black girls, and it is the focus of the next chapter.

These considerations may—and should—lead to questions about how the school, curriculum, lesson plan, and other elements affect the tapestry of Black girls' lives and those of their families. The questions you may have about how and whether to explicitly center conversations, texts, and other materials grappling with racial and gender bias, or what specific actions you may take, should be part of a cooperative, participatory inquiry within your educational community. This inquiry, as a participatory action research project, should not be just for the sake of inquiry but should be implemented toward the goal of co-constructing both the *real* questions that need to be tackled in transforming the school into a location for healing and the development of *real* solutions. This participatory approach can be drawn from the body of participatory action research and transformative scenario planning,[4] which may follow a cyclical process (as shown in Figure 2.1) consisting of the following:

- Co-construction of the research question and development of the "action research team," which must include Black girls, as members of the affected population
- Collective visioning for the desired outcomes
- Design and planning of the specific actions related to the inquiry
- Implementation of action items
- Observation and documentation of the efficacy of actions taken to address the inquiry/issue

- Reflection on the outcomes of these actions and the implications for other actions to be taken toward the goal of eliminating school pushout and its disparate impact on Black girls

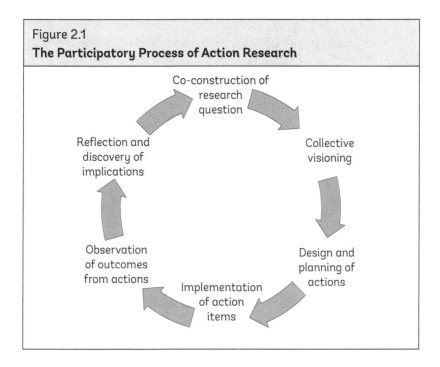

Figure 2.1
The Participatory Process of Action Research

Use of this method can help a school confront some of its hardest questions—questions that cannot be answered through quantitative data alone. The best inquiries are open-ended and specific, invite action and innovation, and require a variety of perspectives to address. The intention must always be to improve conditions. Sample questions include, but are certainly not limited to, the following:

- How does this school cultivate a joyful learning experience for Black girls?
- What actions improve learning outcomes for Black girls?
- How do current disciplinary actions cause or exacerbate harm among Black girls?

- What collaboratives or specific actions reduce the number of suspensions (in-school and out-of-school) among Black girls?
- How can we create inclusive, culturally responsive healing spaces for girls of color in our school?

These and other questions are examples of how a school can engage beyond just accepting trend data as an irrevocable truth. Behind every statistic about school discipline and performance is another action-oriented question that can be answered by a team of students, teachers, administrators, parents, and others (to be determined by the school) who are part of Black girls' village of care in that community.

This kind of inquiry is a basic, nonlinear process that provides opportunities for communities—in this case, the learning community working with Black girls—to better understand itself as a unit, its operations, and its impact (real and imagined) on the learning outcomes of Black girls. This is not a research project on Black girls, but rather a structure to begin mapping the margins to uncover the specific actions that can and must be taken toward increasing the capacity of the school to be a location for healing—and thus a location that works to counter the criminalization of Black girls—and other students—in schools.

3

Grieving the Harms of Institutionalized Bias to Cultivate a Righteous Learning Environment

A critical urban education looks at resiliency and possibility, while not ignoring the stress and strain that urban students incessantly experience. . . . A critical urban education allows us to appreciate the abundance of resources that are available in urban girls' immediate context that may perhaps buffer adversity and further educational resilience among African American female students. . . . [It] also serves the purpose of preparing students to utilize those same support systems to question, critique, and challenge the injustices that they experience as urban girls.

—Venus Evans-Winters, *Teaching Black Girls: Resilience in Urban Classrooms*, Revised Edition

Grieving the harms of institutionalized bias is an important early step toward cultivating school climates that counter the adultification and criminalization of Black girls. For many educators, failing to recognize how deeply rooted many of these harmful social biases are prevents them from fully applying a rigorous analysis to reconciling the situation.

When we think of grief, we often think of losing people, not status. However, to effectively cultivate the scholarship of Black girls, whose sensibilities are routinely tuned in to the mechanics of equity, acknowledging the role of institutions in perpetuating harms is an important activity. It is also important that this activity not be reduced to a single act or collection of rhetorical engagements. Educational institutions—and their agents—must undertake the intense, necessary work of fully grieving the loss of unearned status and privilege that accompanies a full transformation toward equity.

Malidoma Somé contends that the process of grieving is not a solo act, but rather a process that demands the coming together of forces that can help facilitate healing, stating that "healing, ritual, and community—the goods that the indigenous world can offer to the West—are the very things that the modern world is struggling with."[1] This process also offers an opportunity for people to be in deeper community with themselves. Somé continues, "When there is a place for people to listen to the voice of their own emotions, it leads to the opening of a wider door that can allow people to start communing. . . . Feeling is the motor of action. It is the fire that moves us into doing things. It is also the teacher of human wisdom."[2] For school district policy leaders, school principals, and educators, the act of grieving institutionalized bias is necessary in order to fully map the harms of racism on a particular community or school, and to collectively rebuild an educational system that is not designed to sustain oppression but rather to intentionally dismantle it.

The Five Stages of Grief in Educational Institutions

Psychologists refer to Elisabeth Kübler-Ross's five stages of grief as a way to understand the processes by which humans recognize and ultimately heal from loss. The stages are denial, anger, bargaining, depression, and acceptance. *Denial* may involve avoidance, confusion, elation, shock, and fear. *Anger* may involve frustration, irritation, and anxiety. *Bargaining* may involve struggling to find meaning, reaching out to others, and telling one's story. *Depression* may involve feeling overwhelmed or helpless, experiencing hostility, and fleeing from the problem. *Acceptance* may involve exploring alternative options, putting a new plan in place, and moving on.[3]

These stages are now commonly understood to be dynamic and non-linear. We also recognize that not everyone will experience every stage the same way—or at all. However, they offer some guidance on how educational institutions may potentially grieve their role in the tapestry of harm in Black girls' lives—and begin healing, through accountability. In educational institutions, grieving the dismantling of institutional bias may manifest differently than if one were grieving the death of a loved one.

Denial of institutional bias in educational settings may certainly involve avoidance, shock, and fear. However, it may also include actions taken in developing school curriculum, professional development, and other school-based activities that deny the importance of addressing how schools have historically harmed Black girls. The disregard is a form of intentional neglect that impedes the process of repairing the relationship among Black girls, their families, and the institution.

Anger associated with dismantling institutional bias may involve frustration and irritation, but it is almost always associated with a fear of losing privilege and, for some, anxiety about being perceived as a racist institution. This fear can contribute to actions that intentionally undermine or sabotage the success of efforts designed to address racialized gender bias in schools.

Bargaining related to the dismantling of institutional bias may involve a struggle to find meaning, but it may also involve attempting to negotiate and engage in the development of hierarchies—arguing that the centering of one group is "practical" or consistent with "traditions" that leverage the privilege of one group while erasing other groups.

Depression in response to dismantling institutional bias in educational settings certainly involves feeling overwhelmed, but it may also be accompanied by apathy, which facilitates a failure to respond. Some institutions claim that participation in oppressive structures is a function of expediency—they don't have the time (or incentive) to actively dismantle the oppressive elements of their learning structure or curriculum. Some institutions may even argue that it's just "too big" an issue for their size and scope in the U.S. educational landscape. Dismantling institutional bias is a large task if undertaken all at once, and the sense of being overwhelmed can, again, lead to "active inaction."

This acknowledgment of the five stages of grief is not to suggest that these stages occur without harm to Black girls and other students. These actions can render ineffective the efforts to cultivate schools as locations for healing. Although these phases of grieving may be part of the process, it is important to structure responses to ensure that schools, and the educators who work with Black girls and other girls of color, do not remain stagnant. Ultimately, accepting the need to dismantle institutional bias is the breakthrough we are seeking. As facilitators of learning, schools must become locations committed to equity for *all* students, not only Black girls. Equity is a central element of becoming an environment that is safe enough for all students to learn.

Although some may begin with acceptance and then work through the other stages as they actively examine policies and practices, it is essential to understand that cultivating the Black girl scholar is about more than just representation in conversation and curriculum. It is about co-constructing an environment that facilitates care when walking through this grief. It is also about responding with love when Black girls are not shy in their gifts—when they express their desire to lead, their capacity to articulate policies that may trigger a school's grieving process or may signal that the institution's psychological reign as a basic tool of white supremacy may be ending. It is about seeking remedy when Black girls articulate how schools are functioning as part of the tapestry of harm in their lives. Their "challenging behavior" is often an acknowledgment of their gifts—even if unstated—and may trigger retaliation unless the school has developed an infrastructure to walk with them on this journey rather than fight them along the way. Venus Evans-Winters and I talked about what this might look like.

MONIQUE

What is your observation about what happens in schools when Black girls are not shy in their gift?

VENUS

When Black girls are not shy in their gift, I would say that as far as K–12 education is concerned, they are typically punished. They are punished and penalized into submission. They're punished, meaning that many of our girls are taught at home, and in their communities, to show up as leaders and full participants in their households. However, once they enter a school building, they're told to be quiet: "Don't be so loud!" "Stop talking." "Listen and sit down." All of these very submissive gestures that at home they would actually be punished for . . . and I don't mean punished in the way that is oppressive, but in a way that says, *If you do not speak up, if you do not talk for yourself, if you do not protect yourself and others, then you will be taken advantage of [there will be consequences]. . . .* So, to do their part, parents say, *I'm going to teach you how to show up whole, to speak up, to participate, to have confidence and esteem.* So I think as far as K–12 education, when you bring that part of your Black girl identity to school—even though it is part of your identity within your larger family household, and also the community—it causes this type of dissonance. Black girls begin to ask themselves, *Who am I? Here, I'm punished; there I'm rewarded.* So it teaches you to shrink into submission or be punished.

MONIQUE

This reminds me of the adage "A closed mouth don't get fed." To be clear about that tactic, survival in some of these educational spaces can certainly mean that you have to speak up or you are confused into shrinking yourself or bringing only part of yourself to your learning, which creates a condition of unsafety. From this, we might begin to conceptualize how much Black girls who live so fully in their body, live so fully in their voices. Or they fully embrace themselves—their gift—and take the punishment in a way that may lead to other problematic outcomes.

In your work, you've spent a lot of time unpacking resilience and Black girls in schools.[4] How do you think schools can see Black girl resilience as an asset rather than punishing them for it?

VENUS

I think, first, we have to reclaim the term *resilience*. I think that it's been stolen, co-opted, in the same way that trauma is being stolen and co-opted, and in the same way that our call for access to fair and equitable education became No Child Left Behind, which started to punish us for what we had been asking for: school accountability. We *want* teachers to teach all of our children regardless of race, gender, or IEP status. But we woke up to our kids being pulled out, snatched out, and isolated and fingered as the causes of failure.

We know that for Black girls, resilience is adapting to whiteness inside of classrooms when necessary, but also retaining Blackness in order to retain a "righteous mind" and to do good by other students. A Black girl may get kicked out of class, do her time—three days out—come back to school, and still make the honor roll. Nowadays everybody's talking about grit. We understand the idea of resilience as being able to take a hit and get back up. But we haven't been talking about resilience as a resistance strategy. Black girl resilience and our resistance strategies are culturally relevant, very culturally specific. Resilience, therefore, is getting back up by drawing upon your own internal resources and the resources around you. I've really become concerned that the resilience conversation has been co-opted and gutted of the *resistance* aspect. Black girls' resilience doesn't always conform to white supremacy, and it doesn't conform to white femininity. That's the issue.

MONIQUE

In my lectures and writing, I've talked about advocacy as a critical part of creating schools that are locations for healing with Black girls. Our girls often don't feel whole without the capacity to be engaged.

That's one of the critical ways that we begin to articulate our location and to challenge this notion that the Black body is problematic. That's where the resistance that you're talking about is celebrated. I go around and invite people, and to schools especially, to think about how they spend all of Black History Month telling us about Black forms of resistance and spend Women's History Month celebrating strong women who challenged the submission of women . . . and then punish the girls in real time for doing the same thing. It sometimes brings people to a moment of pause, because they're not used to thinking about their own actions in that particular context, or the acts that we are now claiming to be part of that spirit of resistance, the advocacy, as being a critical part of the pedagogical approaches used to engage Black girls. They tend to think of it as something separate, something extracurricular; but really it has to be curricular—central. It has to be embedded in the way we are teaching what we are teaching and how young people are learning.

VENUS

Can I follow up on that? I critique the co-optation of resilience as it appears to put all of the responsibility of success or failure on the Black girl. In my work, *I* may have started with resilience and coping factors to buffer stressors, but then *you* came and started talking about advocacy and protection. So what I'm starting to see now—and I'm wondering if you're seeing this also—is that the pendulum has swung. Now I get these calls, or we do the talks, and we have more Black women and white women—even some Black men—who are starting to protect Black girls in our schools. They're advocating for them by standing up and saying, *Well, is that really what you saw?* when a girl is in trouble. You know, they're saying that to another teacher or to a school or a resource officer. They're saying, *Well, you know what? Maybe this wasn't right, but what can be an alternative to punishment, right?*

So we went from *resiliency* of the Black girl to *protection and advocacy*. But we're missing that middle ground where we have to give Black girls spaces to learn how to now advocate and protect *themselves*, and other Black girls if necessary. We don't want to strip Black girls of that sense of agency that facilitates resiliency. We don't want them to be passive in our liberation struggle.

MONIQUE

No, we don't.

VENUS

We want to get them to do what they're supposed to do in oppressive systems, which is to resist in their own ways, so that one day they can evolve to become a leader in their own schools, their own hospitals, their own country.

MONIQUE

What's also interesting is that I think it's mostly because people are still having a difficult time understanding what Black girlhood is, and what the [unique] contributions are of Black girlhood to our public discourses on justice. So folks can only conceptualize this idea where either they have to be the *strongest* and most resistant to oppression, or we stand in the way, rather than thinking about the language we used around the *Pushout* documentary, which was #STANDING*WITH*BLACKGIRLS and engaging them in a conversation about the mobilization of their own communities. We have to spend some time dealing with the structure of school, so that when girls are standing in their space, or when they are speaking their mind, they're able to cultivate themselves in accordance with the things that will help them thrive.

You said something earlier about the "righteous mind." And instantly I was like, *OK, how are we thinking about classrooms and schools such that they cultivate the "righteous mind" rather than the "colonized mind?"* We know the colonized mind and the way that schools are structured to feed into it.[5] It's what strips so many Black girls of their agency, strips so many Black girls of being able to see themselves in the curriculum, in the school environment, in a meaningful way. So how do we cultivate the righteous mind in your practice in work, rather than the colonized mind?

VENUS

You know, what's interesting, there is a body of research that most people either ignore or overlook. There's research that shows that when you have gender-specific schools, all-girl schools, all-Catholic schools, etc.—and this is at the college level and K–12—they tend to actually outperform their peers that aren't in gender-specific schools. Girls in girls-only schools tend to become top leaders in their field. That can be in politics . . . as in Hillary Clinton. It can be in math; it can be in science. They tend to go into nontraditional fields for women. Then you look at this other body of literature on African American children, or independent Black institutions, and you also see data similar to the gender-only girls' schools. [In well-resourced Black schools], you'll see higher self-esteem; you'll see increased numbers in leadership roles or with positive feelings about their leadership capacity. In these schools, Black children do well in math, science, and reading. They're more likely to go on to college or even grad school and outperform their same-race peers—or even their white peers or higher-income peers. We have to bridge these worlds. There's no excuse that we don't have enough research or literature on the Black girl schooling experience.

So can we reimagine a curriculum that centers Black girls, Indigenous girls, and [other] girls of color and women? What does that look like for our Black girls and other girls of color, and all children in our schools? Imagine if we had known the history of Kamala Harris before she rose to the White House? Imagine that! What if we knew her story before she rose to the top? What if we knew her mother's story as an Indian immigrant who came here as a college student on a visa or [her father's story as] a dad who was Jamaican and came to the United States to become a professor? Then imagine if we also knew the story of Coretta Scott King. What if we knew, just like we know the names of people like Piaget and Erickson, the name of Septima P. Clark? What if we knew Gwendolyn Brooks not as a marginalized story or an isolated name taught during Women's History Month or in an elective course? What if people heard of Black feminism before they went to graduate school?

Can you imagine not hearing about Martin Luther King Jr. until you went to graduate school? We don't hear of Assata Shakur until graduate school—or even after graduate school. This colonial education not only impacts us racially, but it impacts us from a gender perspective. I read Winnie Mandela's story in middle school because I was one of the few Black girls in class, and I was really interested in reading stories about Black people. I was a bad-ass . . . I couldn't keep my name off the board! And then a white teacher simply started giving me books: Winnie Mandela, Nelson Mandela, and Desmond Tutu. It just took me down another road. She clearly saw something in me, this white teacher, that I didn't even see in myself. She knew that I could get lost. But imagine if every girl was given a book like that in middle school, or even elementary school, as part of the core curriculum.

MONIQUE

You know, similarly, I had a white teacher who saw something in me too. And the model was not, *Oh, here's a Black girl I need to save.* Her intention was not to say, *I have all the answers, and therefore, I'm going to show her the ways of living so that she can conform to the things that we know will make her successful in life in "my" world.* The intention was, *I see a potential skillset.* She identified skillsets in me, and she took those skillsets and helped me hone them. I love her to this day.

These teachers said or did things that would allow us to take agency in our own lives, by having a greater command of a history and narrative that *we* thought was valuable. To me, that is partly how we get to this cultivation of the righteous mind. But I feel like, in order for us to get there, school systems as we know them are going to have to grieve. They're going to have to grieve what it is to lose the power that comes from the colonial model.

Can we talk about that for a minute? Because I think a lot of what you write about, what I write about, and what others practice and write about, it's really about coming to terms with what the schools are going to have to *lose*. So what do you think schools will lose when they release the old models that we know have fostered bias and discrimination in the learning community?

VENUS

I love that question. I work in the area of trauma, loss, and grief. I want to apply that model to respond to your question.

What does loss or grief look like? First, there's denial. Who died? Who left me? Who got hurt? What are we asking schools as institutions to give up? They're going to have to deny their inherited supremacy. That's first and foremost. They'll have to get past the denial phase of loss, get past that "white is right and everything else is wrong" mentality. Or "white is superior and Black is inferior." Or "Indigenous is backwards." . . . And then after denial, of course, they're going to have to go through this phase of anger . . . be pissed, be upset. They'll be mad that someone is killing their dreams. These lies that they were fed that white people are superior—religiously superior or morally superior, aesthetically superior, and intellectually superior. Could you imagine that kind of anger? We're talking about 600–700 years of psychosis.

So they're going to be upset; they're going to be angry. We're seeing a moment right now with it. I mean, that's why you got people storming the Capitol, interrupting school board meetings. They're angry, because we're challenging their psychology and their superiority. It is not the first time the status quo is being challenged; but, you know, grieving is a shift of going back and moving forward.

And so finally we will get to the phase of acceptance of the loss of the colonizers' education system. So a part of that acceptance stage would be among our teachers, our political leaders, even our textbook writers. Just accepting the fact that, wow, we have a diverse human experience here in the United States. And globally, everyone has contributed to the American imagination, or the human experience. So how do we accept that? And what does that look like, curriculum-wise, now? . . .

We're going to go through probably some depression before acceptance, depending on where you are. So those in power got to be sad and cry guilty tears. But we don't need your *guilt*; we need your *action*. And so only before we go through those four or five phases—again, depending on where you're at and where one is at in their racial consciousness—then we can have acceptance, healing, growth, and collaboration that's meaningful.

MONIQUE

That's important to lay out, because a lot of people want the acceptance and the partnership without having gone through the steps of grieving and accountability. That's why we see people adding piecemeal components to the school learning environment, like the electives and the extracurriculars, thinking that they're building out a space without acknowledging that the core curriculum is still in the colonial model. By adding others this way, all you're just saying is, *Oh yeah, and you too.* Students feel that, and they know that they are seen as an optional addition rather than something central to the narrative, or actually understood to be co-constructors of the narrative.

VENUS

The system is what holds these ideologies and false narratives. We have to keep in mind that part of that grieving process will not only be for our white peers; it's also going to be for some of us [Black people]. Many of us are suckling at the udder of white supremacy, and we got Stockholm syndrome. So we're going to have to deal with that.

So, Monique, you're talking about the system, and that's interesting to me. In African psychology, we definitely start with the system, which is the European model of colonialism. They set out to conquer the world, the globe, human life, plant life, and water—all of that. But we also must look at the micro or interpersonal. So that's the individual level, and that's where there is going to be some of the white guilt. That's where we're going to experience Stockholm syndrome. Unfortunately, that's the hardest part of justice work and decolonizing education at any given time. We're trying to dismantle, repair, reimagine, and heal.

MONIQUE

For me, fundamentally, I believe girls have to be a part of that. Even in systems and structural levels, you start to see people trying to build out opportunities for input in these spaces. It has to be much more robust. If we're going to actually reimagine what it could be, we have to include them in that process. They can help us imagine what schools *gain* when they release the model of colonization.

VENUS

What they're going to *gain* is diversity in human talent. If you look at the American educational system, it's not working for the majority of the students. And even for those students, those middle-class to high-income white students who it is supposed to be working for . . . when you look at the data of their performance internationally, the United States is actually being outperformed. So, to maintain white supremacy, we're actually losing across the board.

MONIQUE

The U.S. commitment to racism has lost the United States $16 trillion.[6] I mean, even though economic growth is not the sole measure of success, what more do people need? Mend that broken model. The only thing that it serves is a false sense of identity and a weird commitment to a racialized idolatry that just doesn't do anything but feed the broken egos of hurt people. I'm not a psychologist, as you are, but when I think about these things, I'm seeing that "hurt people" hurt people. And the level of structural hurt that we see perpetuated in so many systems—but particularly in educational systems, which we turn our children over to—is something that we have to actively address. Because the hurt people, who are creating hurt systems and information that then feeds into this perpetuation of hurt, are not serving us well.

VENUS

And I would say, to add to your analysis, it also gives this country a false sense of security. And that's actually scary for me, because it's making all of our children vulnerable. For example, environmental racism is real right now in Flint, Michigan, even in Appalachia, in Virginia. I mean, this is real. I wrote a white paper looking at some of the behavioral issues in our schools and their relationship to the environmental aspects of racism. We need to talk about behavioral issues and what kids are learning and not learning, and we need to consider things such as high levels of lead in the water supply too.

MONIQUE

Or even how climate change is impacting actual weather, which increases the vulnerability of our girls and their learning communities.

VENUS

All of this is interconnected. What can be gained from more humane schools? Schools would gain more qualified teachers. And by "qualified" I don't mean who passed the test or who graduated with the right credentials. I mean people who are culturally affirming, those who can also protect the dignity of the child and counter dehumanization—you know, the humanity of students. Our Black teachers are "leaking" through the teacher pipeline, leaving and being pushed out of the pipeline early on in their careers. So we'd gain retention.

We would gain more engineers. Math is actually tied to confidence. So that's why white boys are able to dominate in that space. It's not because they're smarter. You will have more Black girls who are interested in math simply based on confidence. Recent data show us how Black girls actually have a higher capacity for leadership than other girls. We know self-esteem data has been there for a while. But now we're talking about school leadership. Now we're just talking about cultivating a more compassionate citizenry, so we're more likely to look out for other people, like the elderly and people who have been incarcerated, for example. Black women and girls have an ethos of care; so, there's that to gain.

I remember when the Kaiser Permanente report[7] first came out, Monique. I saw those ACEs [adverse childhood experiences] scores, and

I saw where the data was collected. I thought, *Whoa, we have a mental health problem in this country.* And ground zero is the adults. Yep. It's the adults. So, you talk about grieving and healing, and where do we start? Of course, we have to diagnose the system first, but we also have to look at the people whom the system has put in charge of our children. The truth is, we're all screaming about ACEs; and I think the ACEs assessment is OK, but considering ACEs alone is not the solution. In my business, it's a starting point.

So when I looked at the shared ACEs results of that original study, I thought, *Oh, we have a trauma problem in the United States.* I thought of [author and educator] Joy DeGruy. She looks at transgenerational trauma and post-traumatic slave disorder. The slave modus operandi didn't only hurt Black people. It hurt African people and white people. We see in the United States, we have a problem with substance abuse, alcohol addiction, child abuse, and also domestic violence. So, knowing this, and starting to think about where our teachers come from—because our teachers are typically from more vulnerable backgrounds, and they're young, compared to the general population and other professions—I really do think that our white teachers need to be given more opportunities to turn the mirrors on themselves. Now don't get me wrong. People like Paulo Freire and bell hooks have called for critical self-reflexivity in teacher education, but somehow that became so superficial and disconnected from the necessary skillsets teachers should possess.

MONIQUE

When I used to do professional development, I would spend a lot of time on ACEs. I did it just as a way to introduce educators to the concept. And also, I would invite educators to unpack the emergent neuroscience about the brain, and how the brain relates to behaviors associated with feelings of safety or threat. People would always say, *You came to talk about Black girls. Why are you talking about trauma and the hemispheres of the brain? And why are you talking about why it's important for us to unpack our own ACEs?* Then they'd get it. We need to cultivate schools that are responsive to trauma; and to do that, we must be familiar with our own. Representative Ayanna Pressley has put together a package of policy documents and potential legislation that would even invite schools and support their capacity to have conversations about ACEs because of the "hurt people, hurt people" idea.[8] And unless we are really actively engaged in something beyond the rhetoric of critical reflection, we'll get nowhere. It's hard work to continue to turn the camera on yourself and the mirror on yourself.

VENUS

I say that we need to heal as a nation. If we have more data and substantial narratives about who is being put in charge of our children, then we can know how to fix the system.

MONIQUE

How can grieving and healing in this context be seen as an act of self-reflection, not just for those who are responsible for cultivating the space as adults, but also the girls themselves? And how are we thinking about where there might be opportunities to reimagine what's possible even with the curriculum? Too many of us in education are vigilant defenders of a narrative that really only benefits a normative, cisgender, hetero, white, middle-class malehood. I think it is really steeped in a privilege of certain kinds of knowledge.

The bottom line is, how do we do the repair work? A lot of people are like, *I don't send my kids to these schools; we have our own schools.* But what does that mean for public education? How do we move the public education conversation forward, toward a space of healing, particularly from its racism?

VENUS

What comes to mind is a tool and a methodology. I think one tool is the United Nations Committee on the Rights of the Child. So, elevating the *human rights* of children. The United Nations gives us guidance on what children should be able to learn throughout their childhood. And I think that's our starting point. I think it is our starting point as a tool, as a guide. Then I think we move methodologically to what we saw in South Africa: truth and reconciliation. Of course, it wasn't a perfect process, but it gave people the opportunity to share their side of the story.

Could you imagine that Black girl—little Serena, Wanda, or Rayneesha, even a girl who's been previously pushed into the juvenile detention center or foster care—sitting down with that white teacher and saying, *Let's tell our truths. Now, how can we heal together?*

Your work has looked at the restorative justice circles, and we both know too many restorative processes and protocols have been gutted of their original meaning and purpose. Too often it becomes about the child saying, *I did wrong. I'm sorry, Miss Smith. I'm going to do my three-day suspension, but can I come back into your class*? That's when I have to remind adults in schools that's not what "restorative practices" means. It means that there was a problem in the school environment, in a learning context, and a violation occurred in the environment; and now you both have to talk about how best to solve the problem. How do we work together to repair the community or fix the climate that led to the violation in the first place? Restorative practices were never meant to be about one person taking the blame and the punishment, or to be about ignoring what was going on before the act occurred. So, could you imagine a space that's more gender-specific and culturally relevant as it relates to restorative practices?

Maybe we wouldn't even call it that, because we've always had to evolve our language as a people just to keep ahead. How can we bring truth to reconciliation with the human rights of children in mind?

MONIQUE

I actually started this whole inquiry with that question. It was probably 2010, and I would just call a group of sisters, including folks like Fania Davis, the founder of Restorative Justice for Oakland Youth, over to discuss how we can make restorative justice work for Black girls. At the time, the question was really a local one, because the local data were showing that Black girls were not participating in restorative justice programming. When they did participate, they were not particularly satisfied with their participation in it. Since then, it's kind of been an ongoing open inquiry for me. Practice is good, but we're still missing a piece of it, and it doesn't capture what Black girls *need* in order to feel like there has been a repair of relationships—especially the most important relationship of all: the one with ourselves.

How do we facilitate processes that engage girls in helping us figure out what that should look like? I've explored it, and I see elements of art in it, elements of care and mothering in it. If a girl gets jumped by another girl and she has to come back to school the next day and look at the girl who jumped her in the face, what is required here? In addition to having a chance to *talk* about it (in circle or otherwise), some girls needed to detox or to process why she was fighting in the first place. Some girls needed stable housing to regulate their behaviors, or to resolve the harm.

This is what makes ending school pushout and connecting with communities to support Black girl excellence a structural concern. How do we bring forth a reconciliation process that allows educational institutions to grieve their location in the narrative of white supremacy while working to dismantle the other systems of oppression, particularly in the lives of Black girls?

Takeaways for Your Practice

Cultivating a righteous learning environment begins with countering the adultification of Black girls. Educators and other adults in schools routinely work with children and adolescents whose physical attributes and emotional maturity span a wide spectrum. In their classrooms are young people who grow from small children to adolescents—each in a process of *becoming*. Yet Black girls are often viewed by educators—and others in the school environment—as less innocent and childlike than they are.

The foundational study on adultification and Black girls by the Georgetown Law Center on Poverty and Inequality found that African

American girls experience a specific type of age compression in which they are seen as more "adultlike" than their white peers.[9] Black girls, according to the findings, are perceived to need less nurturing, less protection, less comfort and support, and to know more about sex than their white peers. The study also found that the disparity in treatment begins when girls are as young as 5 years old, and that perceptions of difference are at their greatest when girls are between the ages of 10 and 14.

Researchers from the University of California, Berkeley, and the University of Oregon have found that although adolescents are starting puberty earlier, their brains are also responding to stimulation from the adults and peers in their lives in ways that shape their maturation and the trajectory of their social and physical well-being.[10] In other words, what we believe about young people matters—it informs how we treat them and what they come to believe about themselves.

Specifically, treating a Black girl as though she is older than she is can have several negative outcomes, including the following.

Immediate censure when girls make a mistake. Black girls who have participated in my research, as well as those profiled by others, report that they feel educators have "less patience" with them when they make a mistake or do not understand instructions and expectations. Black girls have shared that when they arrive late to class, for example, they are immediately and officially reprimanded, whereas their counterparts from other racial groups are treated with more leniency. Black girls have also shared that they observe educators patiently answering questions from other students, but when they come forward with their questions, they feel rushed or treated as if their inquiries are a bother. And then there are the incidents of harsher treatment—removal from the classroom, suspension, and corporal punishment where it is legal—for comparable behaviors that result in their counterparts receiving warnings or informal interventions to correct.

If a girl is believed to be older than she is, the censure is immediate, and her assertions of independence, peer pressure, or other lapses in sound judgment are not viewed as consistent with her chronological or developmental age; rather, they may be seen as violations of a social order beyond the maturation of that student. In New York City, girls asked for "less metal detectors and more authority figures who care about the well-being of our children," largely because they felt unfairly targeted by instruments of surveillance.[11] When we believe someone "should know better," then we are more likely to respond punitively and less inclined to provide opportunities for girls to learn from their mistakes through discussion, counseling, and guidance.

Hypersexualization and differential enforcement of school codes of conduct. The belief that African American girls know more about sex or are participating in sexual activity at an earlier age than their white counterparts informs how educators—and others working in schools— interpret the sexuality of Black girls and sexual activity (consensual or not) on campus. In my work, I have encountered teenage girls who describe how school security personnel and other adults on campus have made comments about the shape of their bodies, in the context of dress code enforcement or in other scenarios. In Washington, DC, where African American girls are nearly 18 times more likely than their white peers to be suspended,[12] Black girls describe the dress code in their schools as "unequally enforced" and "racist, sexist, unfair."[13] For example, dress codes that ban "cornrows, Afros," and other hairstyles traditionally worn by people of African descent or subjective interpretations of a student's outfit as provocative or inappropriate may be informed by racial bias.

In an egregious (yet true) scenario in California, a group of teenage girls once described to me how views about their sexuality rendered them vulnerable to being sex-trafficked by an adult on the campus of their high school or led to other inappropriate relationships with adults on campus. One young woman shared that the person who introduced her to the underground, abusive world of sex trafficking was the security guard who helped to enforce student dress codes on her high school campus.

Accountability that is more inclined to include punishment, arrest, and exclusionary discipline. When a school's primary mode of intervening involves exclusionary discipline, the opportunity for other measures of accountability are limited. This situation is particularly true for students who are perceived to be older than they are. The infrastructure and climate of a school may begin to reflect criminal legal systems, in nomenclature and sometimes in actual design of facilities. Across the United States, African American girls are disproportionately excluded from participation in restorative approaches and alternatives to exclusionary discipline because their actions may be subjectively determined to be more "defiant" or intentionally disruptive to the learning environment—even though there are important successes associated with their participation in restorative programming.[14]

As I have stated earlier, education is not a neutral act, and educators, like everyone else, hold on to biases. Our collective goal in the classroom is to educate students so that they are prepared for the next level of academic inquiry and to increase their capacity to be effective citizens. How our schools do this important work is informed by all that we bring to our own command of the content that we are teaching, as well as our beliefs in the promise of students. Our pedagogical practices and policies that guide school culture reflect our explicit understandings about the performance and capacity of students, but they also reflect many of our unconscious biases and latent understandings about the conditions and norms that shape identities.

Addressing the adultification of Black girls is hard work, but, given their influence on student development, educators are in a unique position to prevent this phenomenon from having a negative impact on our girls' learning outcomes. Whether in classrooms, on schoolyards and playgrounds, or during informal interactions, we can collectively reduce the presence of adultification in learning spaces by doing the following.

Use Age-Appropriate Language

Referring to a 10-year-old girl as a "young woman" is not always about affirming who she will become. It may be a priming (or trigger) for girls to feel that they are no longer in a critical stage of development and worthy of nurturing. Instead, consider referring to girls under the age of 12 as just that—girls. For adolescents, consider promoting their developmental stages as older children, younger and older teens, as emergent so they know that they will be asked to behave as adults in the future, but that they are still developing into who they will become.

Respect Different Communication Styles

Being "loud" or outspoken is not always an intentional disruption and affront to the authority of a teacher. In Oakland, girls have stated, "African American girls are thought of as being loud, but that's because no one wants to hear us. We have to speak up to be heard."[15] It is important for educators to understand that increased volume is sometimes a communication strategy for girls, who experience (or feel) erasure in their learning space, to be *seen,* rather than an act of immaturity or defiance. One of the most engaging strategies for managing this issue is for the educator to work with the students to set the expectations for the class, so that they understand that a high volume may not always be appropriate. In this space, educators work with students to co-construct when a loud noise might be appropriate, when it is not, and how the class will work together to uphold a structure of accountability on this issue.

Schoolwide, educators can address this "erasure" by establishing advisory groups or other programs for girls that help to build community and a positive culture of communication that is consistent with their developmental stage. Such programs must honor girls' maturity level and provide an opportunity for compassion and empathy among educators to guide decisions about how to steer positive youth behavior and development, such that all in the school community can feel safe enough to learn. To that end, they should be led by individuals who have a demonstrated ability to increase the capacity for Black girls to feel empowered in their learning space.

Recognize Adultification as a Specific and Critical Element of Racialized, Implicit Gender Bias

Training and professional development to address implicit bias should include a deep dive into the possibility of engaging intersectionality—a framework coined by legal scholar Kimberlé

Crenshaw to explore how one's multiple identities (race, gender, ability, sexuality, etc.) inform one's relationships with systems, structures, and individuals—to inform educators' relationships with Black girls and other culturally and linguistically diverse students. We cannot assume that policies and practices intended to be race- or gender-neutral remain neutral in impact. When developing bias literacies, or structured decision-making tools to help standardize criteria and understandings of bias, include specific opportunities to discuss racialized gender-based violence toward Black girls and young women. Examine how these elements might manifest in the school community and be reflected in formal policies and informal practices in ways that may lead to the differential treatment of Black girls.

Establish Connections with Girls So That Each One Has an Adult on Campus She Can Go to in a Time of Crisis

An aspect of adultification is the failure to connect—through empathy and cultural competency—with girls who may come from a community or identity group other than our own. As we build positive learning communities, we should ensure that each student has at least one adult on campus who can function as her "safe person," who she can go to when she is in a moment of crisis, and who can work with other educators to emphasize her full identity and opportunities for inclusion.

I understand the "righteous mind" as the state of consciousness in which a liberatory agenda can thrive—one where the students are free to explore, free to embrace their wholeness in learning. In this state of consciousness, safety is paramount. However, this safety is not possible as long as the vestiges of slavery and its dehumanizing legacies remain as part of the learning community. Grieving white supremacist pedagogy is a critical foundation for the free and righteous mind to thrive—for Black girls, other girls of color, and all students.

First, educators must understand that white supremacist pedagogy—those learning practices that acknowledge only (or primarily) European, linear strategies and frameworks for learning—lacks imagination. It is limited by its own enslavement to privileging the learning styles, content, and conditions that benefit the transfer of knowledge—and even the understanding of what is "knowledge" itself—in ways that serve to maintain the idea of white people's dominance over everyone else. Toward that goal, it is important for educators to commit to and invest in culturally relevant pedagogy in order to cultivate righteous minds, not colonized minds, and provide a foundation for grieving white supremacist ideology.

In *Sing a Rhythm, Dance a Blues,* I invite educators to consider how "teaching to the oppression" undermines Black, Latina, and Indigenous girls' success in the classroom. Learning only about the collective, or noteworthy, experience of people from its relationship to white power (in structure, ideology, and practice) relegates Blackness and other identities to a state of deficiency. Investing in the adoption of culturally relevant pedagogy and the development of required (nonelective) content that educates students about the shared narratives that inform their development is an intentional divestment of white supremacist pedagogy. This divestment is a key element to the grieving that must occur in order for schools to transform.

Using the UN human rights model, how can school communities join this effort toward truth and reconciliation? I wish I could answer this question; but honestly, I believe this is still an open inquiry—a work in early progress. There are core considerations, however, that may guide this process such that the work to grieve racism in educational spaces is rooted in the intention of healing.

This effort will inevitably need to engage—you guessed it—a participatory worldview. Yes, here it is again. Grieving one's unearned, elevated status in the structures of dominance requires understanding why the transition is necessary, how it needs to manifest in the local environment, with the community that has been harmed by the previous structure. Engaging a participatory worldview means that exploratory teams are formed that include Black girls, to examine what policies, practices, conditions, and ideas about Black girlhood inform the potential for differential treatment in the school. How has *this* school participated in the adultification of Black girls? How has *this* school reinforced ideas of Black feminine subservience and hyperaggression? What policies are not just having a disproportionate impact on Black girls, but are covertly—and overtly—sustaining notions of Black female inferiority? How do these facilitate their dehumanization and erasure in the learning?

Once these and other questions are addressed, then the school should consider a cooperative inquiry with educators and staff, particularly those of European ancestry (but this is useful for everyone) regarding what they gain from the current structure and what they stand to lose from shifting it toward a more equitable system. Part of this institutional grieving must also consider how the institution will be held accountable for making structural shifts—not alone, but in community. Grieving, and the subsequent repair of relationships that is necessary to advance "righteous" schools that facilitate the "righteous mind"—for Black girls and other students—is not an individual process. It's certainly a process that involves individual reflection, but that must happen with an aim toward the goal of more deeply interrogating how these personal decisions ultimately affect the structures that form learning institutions in the United States. And it's not just about the classroom.

In May 2021, a Black girl on a North Carolina high school softball team was forced to cut her hair after an ultimatum was presented that her braids and beads were a violation of the dress code.[16] Humiliated, she chose to cut her hair rather than leave the game and sacrifice her position on the team and statistics that might affect her collegiate scholarship opportunities. This is a prime example of how the rules of the game—which may be facially race- and gender-neutral—codify anti-Black standards that disproportionately affect girls. Who wears beads in their hair? Typically, Black girls. This incident, and others like it, invite the question, are her beads interfering with her ability to play? Were these rules developed with consideration for the potential impact on populations who disproportionately wear beads in their hair? Were these communities involved in a discussion about safe ways to contain and prepare their hair so as not to interfere with play?

Also, it's worth noting that institutions need to complete the grieving process—however that looks for them—before launching into action designed to remedy inequity. As this chapter has described, the grieving process is not linear and must embrace the possibility that it may take centuries to recover from the historical trauma produced by decades of living with the harmful misperception of schools as neutral players in the orchestration of society's priorities. It is important to understand schools as part of the structure of dominance, which I discuss in *Pushout* as justification for schools to take a position. Either they will be part of maintaining the status quo of inequality, or they will actively work to dismantle it. Either they will be part of the tapestry of healing or part of the tapestry of harm. Either they will be actively antiracist, or they will operate as racist institutions. There is no neutrality on this issue. Indeed, it is a privilege that educational institutions—and all who are part of that ecosystem—must acknowledge and ultimately release.

So while schools are grieving the loss of their status as an agent of white supremacy and *misogynoir*,[17] they are also going to grieve the loss of having the privilege to claim ambiguity on this question. Grief circles, antiracist learning and educator communities, and schools must operate as antiracist institutions, and in order to do so, they will need to engage the ultimate tool of the desire to do the ongoing, necessary work to align actions with the intention of healing from the vestiges of slavery, sexism, and other forms of expression that caused harm in the first place.

4

Pulling Black Girls in to Orchestrate a Joyful Space

When girls are in crisis, you have to pull them in closer, not push them away.

—Monique Morris

I offered the statement that introduces this chapter as part of my 2018 TEDWomen talk on how Black girls experience school discipline and how we can course-correct toward equity. I've repeated it countless times since then, inviting educators and other adults raising or working with our girls to explore what a "girl in crisis" looks like—and how we can respond to her in ways that facilitate healing rather than harm.

This statement bears repeating because over the past two decades, educators and others who are part of the educational ecosystem have been indoctrinated with the idea that cleaving students from their community is the best way to combat harm. Our policies have prioritized articulating the behaviors and actions that justify marginalizing and isolating youth who have been harmed from their communities without acknowledging that girls who are disruptive are girls who have experienced disruption.

The paradigm shift I am calling for is rooted in the notion that being in community—not in isolation—is what facilitates repair. To bring girls into the work of repairing elements in their lives that can exacerbate harms inflicted onto them (e.g., adultification; sexual, physical, and emotional violence; poorly resourced institutions; biased decision making), they have to believe that their learning spaces invite them in *unconditionally*. Adults—educators and others—must see the activation of effective learning spaces for Black girls as an act of resistance to oppression. We must build institutions that understand learning as a joyful experience and that, by pulling Black girls into that space, can claim that they, too, are worthy of joy.

The GrassROOTs Community Foundation, founded by Janice Johnson Dias, is a "public health and social action organization" that invests in community well-being to transform girls, their families, and communities. The foundation's mission is to fund, support, develop, and scale community health and wellness programs for women and girls—particularly those who are impoverished—and to advocate for policies and practices that reduce disparities and foster equity.[1] Anchored in the principles of Ma'at—truth, order, balance, and reciprocity—the foundation emphasizes training to support Black girls at the intersections of their mental health, physical health, sexual health, and the economics of health to build an ecosystem that advances Black girl excellence.

In 2015, Janice Johnson Dias's daughter, Marley Dias, founded #1000BlackGirlBooks, a national campaign to introduce literature with Black girls as central protagonists into schools. The absence of Black girls as main characters in the books she was required to read left more than just a bad taste in her mouth. Marley asked:

> How can educators expect kids to love, instead of dread, reading when they never see themselves in the stories they're forced to read? . . . If there are no Black girl books as part of the school curriculum, then how are we expected to believe all the stuff that teachers and parents are constantly telling us about how we're "all equal"? . . . If black girls' stories are missing, then the implication is that they don't matter. I didn't like it, so I had to do something.[2]

What began as a mission to collect and distribute 1,000 books with Black girls as main characters grew to more than 12,000 as of this publication. Supported by a family and community that firmly supported her vision to place her gift at center stage and to articulate representation in literary works as part of how justice manifests in schools, Marley is a powerful example of the force that lives in Black girls. The clarity of her vision may not be readily observable in many adolescents her age, but let's not reduce her power to a label of "extraordinary" or "adventurous." Though she possesses a special quality, her interest in learning and being an active force in her community was nurtured by her village—her parents, the GrassROOTS Community Foundation, and her school.

Black girls share that they are ready to lead, but that this readiness and their skills go underrecognized and underutilized in schools.[3] It is important that schools not be an impediment to the realization of Black girls' dreams.

For Marley, GrassROOTS provided a resource that instilled in her the importance of wielding her power for the benefit of her community. In her book *Marley Dias Gets It Done: And So Can You!,* Marley writes:

> Thank goodness for roots. Mine run deep. A couple of years ago, my mom started GrassROOTS Community Foundation (GCF), a public health and social action organization to help women and girls make their lives, families, and communities strong. GCF does some of the most amazing things. Aside from helping to get #1000blackgirlbooks going, GCF is making this planet better by:
> - Developing health and wellness programs for women and girls, particularly those who are impoverished.
> - Training young girls to use their skills and talents to make a difference in the world.
> - Guiding and mentoring Black girls all over the world.
> - Advocating for policies and practices that foster equity.
> - Providing technical support to health and community programs.[4]

I talked to Janice Johnson Dias—Marley's mom—about the core elements of the programming and the underlying philosophy of how to bring Black girls in closer, and what we gain from doing just that.

JANICE

I think about schools as the intersection of community and government; and I often talk about it that way because in America, school is really weird for me. What makes it weird—not bad, but *weird*—is its mandated participation. That's very different from what I knew for the 12-some odd years I lived in Jamaica. This mandated participation, what I assumed by its mandatory nature, is that there would be something else happening, or that there would be different safeguards, different supports, and different understandings, were this not in place. Every time I encounter schools, whether it's the school where I teach at the collegiate level or at the primary, middle, and high school level, there's something just weirdly off about the idea that it's *mandated* while its funding sources are discretionary, its participation is limited, and its engagement is often oppressive.

I think the issue of school pushout came to my attention before. You have to spend 10 years doing the work before people discover you. Those of us in academia who know what is happening, we were already engaged with "pushout." And I just kept thinking about how important it was that it was a reframe. Today I was talking about why I stopped using the term *privilege* and started using *advantage*. And it is because *truancy, detention,* and all the rest of this other language suggested that the actors themselves, the girls, were the problem and that there wasn't a *push* factor.

I come from [a background of] immigration research, in which we're always talking about push and pull factors, so pushout really kind of instantly touched me for that reason. It was the idea that there was a set of mechanisms actually pushing kids out. It wasn't that kids were somehow opting out, which was, I think, the dominant kind of framework for what's been happening. And I rarely hear people talk about that even when they talk about your work and they acknowledge institutional structures. They don't acknowledge that it's really an intellectual reframing of the way we have seen how communities push people out, how government pushes people out, and what happens if there's not a pull factor. There's only a push happening, and then the penalizing for the push. *I'm going to blame you for being pushed out.* Like, *Why didn't you make yourself not move?*

That always kind of sits with me whenever I think about what you have put out there. Maybe people don't realize that it's a reframe, and maybe they're just so happy to have somebody put out work that centers Black girls. But for me, I think a lot of what I'm trying to do with my own work and with my life is to get people to ask different questions and have a different lexicon for how we're thinking about girls, how we're thinking about these things that are at this intersection. So, I come back to pushout a lot, and I see that even with my socioeconomic status, the consistent pushout of kids in general, and this amplification with Black girls. So, I want to just really thank you for that.

MONIQUE

I appreciate that, and I appreciate you too. You're using your work to build on some of these critical questions. And that's really where I hoped people would go with this material. It's not just to say, you know, thanks for writing it, but to really think about what still remains to be interrogated and how we really come together in community. That's why I wanted to talk to you for this project. You have figured out a piece that is not actually super complicated, but it's difficult work around affirming Black girls and their excellence as a healing practice. And the one thing I recognize about you, and I felt it as I was reading through your book, *Parent Like It Matters,* is the need to invest in yourself instead of waiting for other people.

I recognize your commitment to being fully present and expressing joy in almost every opportunity, which I think is so amazing! It's so dope, because you're like, *I am the scholar that I am, but I am the person that I am too.*

JANICE

And try to take that from me! [Chuckles]

MONIQUE

Oh, I'm sure! You know, there's this weird way that we treat learned people and learning environments as if they have to maintain a sterile identity. That, I think, is partly why Black girls get in so much trouble, because we are *not* sterile. I think we are probably asked similar questions because we are raising these amazing girls who do phenomenal things in the community. Some more visible than others, but we're proud mothers of girls, right? And caregivers for girls. We ride hard for girls, which is a little different than even being proud to be a woman or talking about Black women. When we ride hard for Black *girls,* it's a whole other thing, right?

You've spent a lot of time talking about how you poured into the gifts of your daughter. And I've witnessed it for sure with your daughter, but also in your Supergirl camp,[5] where those girls are amazing. You could feel the energy when I visited—and it was a virtual space, so I can imagine what you're pouring out in person! So, let me ask you, what happens when girls are not shy in their gift?

JANICE

I think that the brazen Black girl is hard for everybody—not just for the kind of broader American white society or even broader American Black or Latino society. It's hard for everybody—it's hard for their mamas; it's hard for their daddies; it's hard for their friends. And one of the things that I try to do for our girls is to be that example. Like, I'm hard for people! I try to tell people, *I'm an acquired taste, but I'm good for you.* [Laughs] I'm aspiring.

So, I literally feel like I have to live that for them, for them to see that it is OK. It is OK that you're hard for people. It's not your issue that you're hard for them to digest, because you're good for them, right? Your Black girl confidence and competency is good, which I talked a lot about in my book—this relationship between what happens when your confidence is not coming from your looks, it's coming from your competence. You can read. You can spell. You can do mathematics. . . . How do you retain confidence when people are trying to say, *Wow, you know, it's nice that you're good at that, but maybe you don't want everybody to know that you're good at that.* Well, why not? Other people get to do that.

So, what I do with the girls at GrassROOTS, the girls in my classes, and the friends that I have in my world is remind them that *everybody* else gets to feel great when they're good at something. And if somebody tries to challenge that, then our girls should have a menu of responses to it. Because oftentimes, I think caregivers *want* us to be successful, but they actually don't know the *how.* How do I help you? What's the word you should say when someone confronts you, and why is silence not enough? Like, they'll say, *Mom, they told me that I was too smart.* The response is often, *Well, just don't say anything, baby.* I say, *No, how about you challenge them with information?* Offer to them, *Who do you think is better? Who else has in fact earned this* A *in this class? I actually have. I have the right to claim the spoils of which I have earned.*

So, I really work hard to make sure that our girls are particularly skilled. And people always talk about my obsession with capital transfer and skill development because I want them not to ground their identity in this notion of just having things, but things that are *verifiable!* I want them to have receipts for all of it. And that receipt means that where I find my confidence is not imagined. *I find my confidence in my competency, and therefore, I get to be all kinds of things as it relates to it.* And that's OK.

I show them through my living and through the women who I invite to speak to them. People write to me like, *Can I come to your camp? I'm a motivational speaker.* OK, not interested. What I'm interested in is having girls see Black girls who have grown up into versions of themselves as super competent. They have the right then to be brazen, so they don't feel alone in it. I talk with caregivers and have worked with caregivers a lot, because everyone says they want a competent and confident Black girl, but then when she begins to ask questions, you want to beat her the hell down. Now, the upside of GrassROOTS is that I have kept the foundation super small, even when people have wanted it to be big. So when encounters occur and parents have questions and the girls need support, I can then actually engage in a skill-development module.

I remind them that they said they wanted a confident Black girl, and here she is! You can help her if you don't beat her down like the outside world does. The girls have an ally and a support in me because I'm not theoretical; I'm not historical; I'm not out of their range. I mean, I have to tell you, the girls listen to the women who come and talk to them. After each one of you comes, the girls will be like, *Well, you know, what Dr. Morris said . . .* or *Remember what Michelle Davis said* or *Did you forget what Joanne Smith said?* Like, they feel they now have actual examples, in their real time, that show them it's OK to be competent, brazen, and fly. Those things are really important, and our girls don't get enough examples of that in other spaces, so I try to really craft that space for them.

MONIQUE

I really love that. It's a presentational affirmation, right? I feel like part of what you're cultivating is this sort of representational aspiration and affirmation—just by bringing people into the community.

JANICE

The women who come and the people who in general come to GrassROOTS are people who I feel the girls can reach for. They're in reach. They're not so far out of reach that they cannot feel accessible to them.

My girlfriend says that I craft my spaces. I curate them, and I think that's essential. And that does come from educational research. The educational research that I know, that I don't think suburban Black moms or even Black parents know, is that so many begin by placing their children and their spaces in heterogeneous, hostile environments. And I really strongly know that when kids begin in homogeneous safe spaces, then they can grow first. To have children grow under hostile circumstances is really damaging. So I do the same thing with our girls. *I want you to be brazen now, competent now, foundational now, before you go out there and they try to get you.*

MONIQUE

That's really interesting. Most Black girls are being educated in spaces that are often hostile—repeatedly hostile in both overt and covert ways. And they spend a lot of time in these spaces. And so, largely, one of the reasons that I've located a lot of my work in the educational system is because we need that system to show up differently, even if it can't be the place where that kind of deep, homogenous community and person-building can take place. It needs to at least not undermine the work that is done in other spaces, so that Black girls see themselves and are received as their full selves.

So that brings me to Marley. Because she came on the national scene at 11 years old, right?

JANICE

That's right—at 11 years old. She started to really think about this at 10, and then at 11, she started to say, *Look, I'm sick of [reading about] white boys and [their] dogs, right?* Marley has been an outlier and whisperer for Black and white people in this community for a very long time. And so by the time she was on the national stage, they were like, *I knew something was up with this girl.* People are just like, *Why is she so Black in this white space?* And yet she doesn't sound "Black," because she has the capital exchange, right? So like, it's just been disruptive. She's been disruptive, even when we didn't let her know that this is how white people are reading her, and how some Black people are reading her. She's just been disruptive for them.

MONIQUE

As her mother, what were your conversations with the school when she noticed the absence of Black girl books in the classrooms and libraries?

JANICE

I will say that I had very limited conversations. Marley is the first level, which means, if there's a conflict or *anything* wrong, we armed her with the language for her to advocate within the school. If her advocacy does not work, then we will employ a letter. If it goes all the way wrong, then we will break the glass, and I will then engage them. And usually this occurs in a couple of different ways.

Ever since Marley started school, she is sent on the very first day with a letter from me. That letter says something like, *I am sending you a joyful child, and I ask that you take care of her. Should she come home unjoyful, I will be reaching out to you directly.* My husband has dreaded this letter all through her elementary school years. [Laughs] Marley didn't know what was in the letter. She knew she had an envelope each year, and she had to give it to her main teacher. That has been really important to me, because I told her she had to go to school, because I have to work.

And it's all good, in general. Before she started school, I said, *Look, I don't know anything about American schools. I just want to let you know that my primary interest is my child's well-being. And I get that y'all are going to try to teach her a whole host of stuff. But she's my primary interest.* And by virtue of having a PhD, having this deep, raspy voice, and being 5-feet-10-inches tall, people just generally don't try to f--- with me because they're like, *Mm-hmm, I'm not sure,* right? So that has really worked in her benefit.

By the time Marley's campaign came about, her principal then reached out to me, and he was like, *Well, I wasn't aware. . . .* And I said to him, *Well, how many books do you have in that school?* He said, *You know, I've never thought about it.* So I said, *Well, you know, it would be great if you could tell me if you have a lot of diverse books and what your needs are, because clearly, it's impacted my child.*

And it is largely going to impact the child. When he wrote back, he said he didn't have a lot. And so we gave 1,000 books to that school and brought [award-winning authors] Jackie Woodson and Rita Williams-Garcia there. The white parents had already heard of Jackie Woodson and Rita Williams-Garcia, but the Black parents hadn't. Still, they were just happy to get 1,000 books and to have these two authors at the school. And the school made the book that Marley suggested become the main read for the entire school. Since then, they've made sure that the read is a diverse book going forward.

MONIQUE

That's good. I didn't send my daughters with a handwritten letter; I would just follow everything with an email. It wasn't about sending them a joyful child, because I don't even know if I had that framework available to me. But having grown up in the United States and knowing what U.S. schools were expected to teach, I knew there were certain narratives about their history—and their people—that I wanted to control so that it would be correct. I intentionally put my daughters in a school where they could learn about certain things, like the institution of slavery, from me first. I wanted them to learn those core things from me, not from the school, so they wouldn't think their history begins with slavery, as schools would have us all believe.

When they were 6 and 8, I also had the ability to take them on a trip to The Gambia and Senegal, and we had the discussion about the transatlantic slave trade as a family. We didn't say, *You are the descendants of slaves*. We never used that language. We taught about oppression, and we understood who had the problem. We understood what the issues were, and that's how I sent them to school.

So the conversations I had with educators early on was, *I'm sending you a child who is deeply rooted in her awareness of herself. So there may be times when she challenges you. There may be times where she's inviting a different kind of conversation about this curriculum, and I need you to know that we taught her that. And I need you to know that if you have an issue, please contact us to make sure that this is not something that is used to punish her.*

What's interesting, though, is even in those conversations that I was having with the teachers, and the conversations that I would have with my daughters separately, there were *still* occasions where they would hide things from me, because they knew "the regulator" would show up—I would come! And so, I hear things years later that are like, *I didn't tell you because I knew you would come to school and wreck.* [Laughs] It's interesting how our girls still are in a space where they recognize this institution, though, as a place where they need to engage in some kind of peacemaking.

I love that part in your book where you say you've effectively taught your daughter how to hold forgiveness in times of conflict—even when you, yourself, were ready to wreck. That's why I feel like it's important sometimes to spell out what the schools do well. Speaking of which, what do you think the school did well in their response to Marley's critique of the curriculum?

JANICE

I think that they stayed in it. They were willing to hear me, and this is where I think class and race meet. Because I have the PhD and we're in a middle-class neighborhood with a median household income of $91,000, my words are perceived to have more weight. So they were willing to listen. And that always concerns me because I know that they're not listening to me because I'm somebody's Black mama. They listen to me because I'm Dr. Janice Johnson.

They did try to ask the hard questions, and I don't think that was because of me. I think they were asking themselves the hard questions because there was now a national spotlight, and they didn't want to be *that* school—that school where that little girl is on *The Ellen Show* or *CBS This Morning* saying they wouldn't move. So I think that was it. I also think it brought to their attention the insidiousness of racism's ability to erase you—that *I didn't even think to think of you.*

MONIQUE

You know, the rendering of a population as invisible is a form of neglect and violence.

JANICE

They should think about that. Again, we're in suburbia and Biden-esque America, where people don't want to be racist, and so it made them pause. And I think that their pause, plus the national spotlight, plus a PhD and the fact that I am a really active community agent, made some things move. And I'm not just a PhD, writing across from them as I sit on a commission. I'm also *there*. Unlike other Black and Brown members of our white neighborhood, I'm a blacktop mom. So that meant that they will have to see me on the blacktop too. I don't leave at 7 a.m. and come back at 7 p.m. I'm also there lingering, right? So they couldn't avoid me. I think those kinds of social pressures made the school behave differently. And I think that that's one of the many reasons why some of these urban spaces—some of these other spaces where Black labor-force participa-tion is different than [that of] other advocates who have the luxury of being blacktop moms—get different outcomes. If they're not connected to those groups, then they actually cannot serve kids well.

MONIQUE

There are also parents who don't have the flexibility or who are loathe to be blacktop moms because of their own historical traumas associated with learning and educational systems that didn't—and still don't—appeal to them as places where they *want* to linger. Or some parents see the school as a place where they never want to be present. They send their kid to school because they have to, but they also send their child to school, depending on their own circumstance, with a set of requirements around how they behave socially to protect their minds, bodies, and spirits from assaults rooted in racism, bigotry, and misog-yny—internalized or otherwise. So if somebody calls you out of your name . . . if somebody comes at you the wrong way, make sure you fight back—all of the things to send signals about how a girl is supposed to interpret her time at school, and how she's supposed to guard herself in those environments. They also affect her ability to feel safe and express joy and be *present*. And so, given that, I think about what schools could do to be part of the tapestry of healing, instead of the harm.

I start to think about what a lot of schools could do differently such that they're really creating an environment that *does* provide for young people to abandon some of those things. And you can't do it without some of these considerations about labor-force participation and limitations that inform how schools are interacting with parents, whether they're blacktop moms and dads or not.

JANICE

There's another piece. . . . I talk a lot with a school in Harlem. My friend used to be a part of this school, and a part of what was happening at this school is that kids got kicked out for everything. And every year there's a career day, and he has me come. I'd always think that my career was the wackiest, because every time I go there, people make so much more money than me! [Laughs] And then GrassROOTS had a program in a northern New Jersey high school, and there are a couple of things about the educators there—Black, Latino, and white—that I consistently found disturbing. There are too many people in the field of education who really are interested in regulating kids, and those folks are a real problem. I actually spent a tremendous amount of time trying to figure out how to get those folks out of the educational system. I just really need them to not be in front of kids.

So one year my friend had me come to his school. The school was all Black and Latino, and it had rails and all the rest of the jazz—a typical "scared straight" school. So I'm a teacher there for career day with another person, a stenographer. She made way more money than me. That's why it's indelibly marked in my head. [Laughs] The kids asked about our income, which I felt was a fair question!

She made $120,000 a year, and all she had was a high school diploma. And to me, they were like, *Ma'am, how much do you make?* And I was like, *Significantly less.* [Laughs] And the teacher in the room, even though she was not in front of the classroom (she was at the back of the room), said to them, *Be realistic.*

Now, my friend made me come. I left Jersey, came across the bridge; I parked my car in Harlem. . . . I dressed up in a suit. I'm here to give the good kids "Dr. Janice Johnson." That's what he wants from me, and I can do that! And that woman said "be realistic" about the kids' occupational dreams? Inside of me, I knew something was wrong, because my body temperature rose. I had to rub my hand and be like, *Janice, you know, don't let your body temperature rise.*

So, I was like, *OK. You still have to be here because this is for your friend. This is his real job. You can't act out of pocket.*

So, I said, *Excuse me. Say a little bit more about what you mean about being realistic.* That's my intro, when people say stuff.

She said, *Well, they're not going to get a PhD. They don't have the patience for it. They're not.*

I said, *Tell me how you gathered this evidence? Like, how do you know?* And she was like, *Well, when I was in school, I wanted to do this, that, and the other.* And I said, *Well, if you just indulge me for a few minutes, and just tell me a little bit about what you ended up doing after high school.* And she said that she went to one of the community schools, and then she got her teaching certificate. And she taught elementary school and that's how she got there.

I said, *Could you tell me a little bit about where you've traveled, where you've gone? Some of the things that you've done?* And she was like, *You know, I mostly go back to my home country . . .* and that was a country in the Caribbean. And I said, *Oh, OK.* And she said, *Why do you ask?* I said, *It makes sense now for me why you would say that.*

And then I said, *You're not imaginative. You've done very little, and you assume these children are you. You cannot engender excellence if you do not feel excellent.* And I just turned my damn head.

A part of that is that the school system is attracting a set of educators that are seeking to *regulate,* not educate. People who are unimaginative cannot see that a part of their task is to help these children imagine a new reality. Now, I understand that caregivers come into the system in all kinds of different ways. Some of us come from other countries; some of us come from low wages; some of us have hospital experience; but *the task of this institution is to be beyond that.* And they must have educators and administrators whose eye stays focused on that. You have to have an institutional imperative to be a place of hope and to hire people who are hopeful. Ask them to be excellent!

MONIQUE

I agree that the criteria need to shift. We hired teachers for the EMERGE program in Oakland,[6] which I helped to launch, after they'd come in and actually performed a sample lesson plan for the kids. Delivering a sample lesson is standard, but we asked them not to be evaluated by *us* necessarily, but to have the students then be a part of the interview panel for their teacher. Certainly, it was an intentional shift of power in decision making, but it was also a recognition that they're going to co-construct this environment whether we recognize it or not. And so, if they are going to be co-constructors of their learning space, why not engage them from the very beginning? That way there are some basic understandings and expectations that they have about how they can work *together* in this process of learning—and doing that with joy.

And it's interesting, because, going back to Marley's story, when I heard about the #1000BlackGirlBooks, the first book that popped in my head was *The Bluest Eye b*y Toni Morrison. I thought of *The Bluest Eye* immediately, because of when [Marley] said, *I was tired of reading about white boys and their dogs. Y*ou know, it was the same way that Toni Morrison writes about the developing psychosis of Pecola, the dark-skinned Black girl who can't get out of her mind the Dick-and-Jane children's stories of the 1950s and '60s. In the story, there's this routine way that white, middle-class norms are presented in children's literature to ultimately drive Black children to a state of insanity. There's a reason this book is pivotal. In so many ways, Marley was actively disrupting that narrative in real time. The story of *The Bluest Eye* is a tragic story—and it was tragic for me because I saw myself in Pecola. I remember being that dark-skinned girl who thought that if I just had green eyes, things might be different for me. Were it not for one of my friends being like, *Monique, stop trippin'. You're beautiful the way you are,* who knows if I would have been able to see myself.

So, when I heard Marley's story, I was like, *Wow! What an amazing possibility!* Then I thought about the school . . . and about why it was important to move this conversation beyond just her school. Can you talk a little bit about why it didn't just stay in her school?

JANICE

It was never even a consideration. She saw schools as a reflection of society. Even this morning, when we were talking, she said that somehow schools have been more influential than anything else. And so, I think she feels that if you influence the world, you'll shape schools.

MONIQUE

Not the other way around? That's an important distinction. If you change the schools, you're shaping the next generation. And she's like, *No. Shape the generation, and then you'll form the schools.*

JANICE

Her vision is like, *if I change everything on the outside, then they'll start to just imagine that Black girls matter, and then that will make it to the schools.* Maybe she's been listening to me, because I often work a lot in the imagination space. You have to *imagine* it. You have to imagine change is possible.

MONIQUE

I appreciate that, and I think it's a brilliant offering.

JANICE

I live with her, and I'm always curious about how she's making meaning of the world, because it's so different from how I make meaning of the world.

MONIQUE

My youngest daughter, Mahogany, who's about the same age as Marley, used to replace misogynous language in a song with the term "misogyny." So when she's rapping, she'll say, "misogyny" instead of the slur. The thing is, it has been socially difficult to stand in that space sometimes. Because people are like, *Oh, she is so mad all the time.* Or, *She's so different, because she's paying attention to the lyrics . . . can she just let it go?* And for her, the answer is usually no. She's just like her mother. [Laughs]

I was reading through your book, Janice, and I realized that these little aggressions attack her ability to be joyful and express gratitude to her ancestors in a way that makes sense to her. Only once the demonstrations of summer 2020 were on the news 24/7 were people finally sending her notes expressing that they understand where she was coming from. Now her friends and classmates are like, *That's what Mahogany was talking about. . . .* So it's an interesting moment to watch girls, especially Black girls, stand in this space where the school is their social and intellectual space.

Mahogany would write papers for class uplifting the value of Black lives, and her teachers would respond with some version of "all lives matter." She felt assaulted by having her intellectual work "all lives matter"-ed. Our girls need the school to show up differently for them. They need their educators to be available to them differently, especially if they don't have parents who can help to mold that discussion. Schools need relationships with people who can serve as proxies when parents and teachers aren't able to hold that content.

JANICE

You just touched on so many things. One of the reasons why Supergirl Society [a program of GrassROOTS] has been so valuable for Marley's development is because it was always, *If you're going to have a playdate, it's going to be at the bookstore with Marley.* There were always these undercurrents. As soon as you say something, she's going to sprinkle either some feminist ideology, some Black ideology, and some international framework. Like, *This happens in America, but you know, in Ghana. . . .*

So at GrassROOTS, she had like-minded people around her. But as she's grown into high school, she's kind of outgrown the foundation in the way she engages with it. She's had to search and work so much harder, because Marley could be a popular girl. But she's relatively shy around certain things, and she doesn't want people liking her for her celebrity. So she keeps a really small, intimate group of friends.

She actually loves football, so she has a lot of boy friends who are interested in sports, and so boys have impassioned emotions. It's so much more respected than when girls have impassioned emotions, which is completely opposite when you're an adult, right? Girls are supposed to be easygoing and not have a strong point of view. But she is brazen. She has a strong point of view that she tries to keep to herself, *until . . .* then something captures it. So that has been hard in her social world, and she's still navigating it. The only sentence I say to her is "College is going to be your time."

MONIQUE

That's what I say to my daughter too! It's interesting, because there's this way that I think both of our daughters are so precocious, and not in negative ways. Like, in the ways that have challenged their learning spaces to figure out why they're questioning so much. Being critical thinkers, in many ways, has made people adultify them. The interesting thing is—and we don't talk about this often—when you are a high performer in schools, the school will adultify you for being a critical thinker—particularly when you are a Black girl.

JANICE

When you are bright, you are instantly adultified as a Black girl. Because you have academic competence, a higher level of emotional competence is expected of you. And that just ruins so many parts of you.

One of the things that we don't demand of teachers is that they are aware of the social world. I demand it of my kid, but we don't demand it enough of teachers. So we have teachers who are like, *Well, I don't know anything about what you kids are listening to. I don't know anything about what you kids are watching.* Even in college, one of the prizes is to not own a TV. So, while teachers are disengaged, we just load more onto Black girls. And we have to actively push back.

On one hand, at the beginning of the conversation, I kept talking to you about how important competence is and why I value that, but then you're penalized so heavily for being competent, because the framework of America is always filtering through what is happening with white girls and white boys. And *their* lack of competence is the default category. So anybody who is not that, and doesn't respond like that, has a penalty.

MONIQUE

I talked about that in *Sing a Rhythm, Dance a Blues,* and you talk about it in *Parent Like It Matters.* But it's really important for us to be very aware of and heal from our traumas. And to situate that in the context of the historical traumas that also inform how these experiences take shape in our lives.

I had a conversation with a group of girls in a school once, and I asked them to remember who they are. And one of the girls asked, *What if I never knew? What if we've never known who we are?* And at first, I was devastated. Like, *No, please don't say that.* But then I realized that she was just being honest. A lot of our girls *don't* know who they are. And so, I was like, *Alright then, we have to create space for Black girls to explore who they are.* That is part of what I'm hoping we'll be able to do when we build out a parent-educator community that finally responds to the full needs of Black girls—to be able to instill in our young people the tools they need to *remember.* And some of that remembering will be through the literature they read. Some of that remembering will be through the collective conversations we have. Some of that remembering will be in the form of the dances and music that are being produced and the way that we can intentionally make connections so that they understand the origins.

I feel that it is how we tap into the joy that has been historically stripped from us. And that's the part I struggle with. I struggle with *joy,* even though I know that's how I got through my own ACEs. Like, I love Prince so much that he was my happy place. To this day, if it's Prince-related, I'm there and I'm happy. I don't have to have answers to anything, and I don't have to be somebody's mama. I'm just me listening to some excellent music and singing along and dancing and remembering this feeling that his music taps into. And for a lot of folks, I think being able to identify a legitimate source of joy is really hard. Joy is not associated with how others see Black girls and Black women. It's hard work to tap into that joy yourself, or what you have described as being able to "celebrate yourself," no matter what.

JANICE

My friend talks to me a lot about that, and in *Parent Like It Matters,* I touch on it. There was so much that I wrote around this idea of the gift of abandonment, right? I feel like it's really quite pervasive in Black communities across the globe, this combination of solitude and faith that meets you when you surrender. My grandmother was like a big Anglican, surrender-all kind of person. And I think one of the things that I'm grateful for, as I've gotten to the cusp of 50, is this understanding that surrendering to things sucks. I don't try to pretend things *don't* suck. And I find that, whether it's this racial moment, other moments in life, people want to quickly pivot, they want to quickly forgive, quickly move on. I just am really not that. I'm like, *This absolutely sucks,* and I think that has been a real gift for my joy, because it's left me in a space of a lot of introspection.

That's where competency and social connectedness happen. What are you capable of? And that's what I'm hoping caregivers recognize—that regardless of what has happened, the pain is *not* the end of the story.

MONIQUE

I think resilience is a big factor for Black women. And we learn it young, but also we build up that resistance over time, because the institutions have not historically provided us with spaces to do that kind of work, day in and day out. That's work that has typically happened outside the school, and sometimes outside the home, and instead in other spaces.

So what we have now, and what we're working on now, is a real opportunity to think about an intentional investment in Black girl-hood that promotes wellness and well-being, and not just *survival*. And that's what I think is beautiful about your framework of joy and change-making as inextricably linked. You elevate this notion of practicing reciprocity in a way that, while it's framed around caregivers and parents, I think there's a lot that's transferable to teachers.

JANICE

There's a lot I want to say to teachers. When I think about Black girls in educational spaces, I think this is where Marley has influenced me most. She's really influenced me in thinking about the role of literature and literacy in helping teachers transform—and what that looks like if you're in Iowa, South Dakota, or Compton; if all teachers recognize that if they even considered that Black girls could be centered, what that would mean for the entire educational system. She did that for me. I don't think I thought about that before, because I always used to say to her, *We have a 13 percent problem in the United States.* She said, *What do you mean?* I was like, *We are 13 percent of the U.S. population.* Mathematically, Black people can't be everywhere, but we need to be in everyone's imagination.

MONIQUE

Beyond problematic ways.

JANICE

Yes. Literature that allows for all of us to imagine a Black humanity. I said to Marley, *You don't understand why I find this so problematic.* And she was like, *Well, what's the deal?* I said, *When I adultify you, I'm constraining your humanity. I'm saying that there's one way for you to be, and it is the most inhumane thing we do with Black folks.*

So when we get to see multiple experiences of Black people, and especially Black girls, we broaden the scope of the model, and that's what we need. We need to imagine that Black humanity has depth and breadth in all of these things. We need it. That's the theme.

MONIQUE

If you recognize the pieces that make Marley "exceptional," we realize that she's a whole person, not just a voice for Black girls since then. I saw that happening from the outside. People did the same thing to [student and gun control activist] Naomi [Wadler] when she hit the national spotlight during the March for Our Lives. These are our girls. *They* are who *we* are, and what we can be. We have to see ourselves in each other.

I was talking to a friend yesterday who was once the leader of a gang. And she's since done amazing, transformative work with girls. When I first met her, I was working for a national research institution on criminal justice, and she always teases that I "thought I was cute," because I was wearing stilettos. And I always just say, *OK* . . . because I *was* cute in my stilettos. [Laughs] She was pregnant—and also cute, by the way. But at the end of the day, her fighter saw my fighter, and my scholar saw her scholar. And that is how we became sisters. So how we position the "outstanding" and joyful Black girl against the brazen Black girl is problematic, both in and out of schools. It has to do with our lack of capacity to see each other in ourselves. I think part of the work here, then, is about how educators can tap into that part of themselves. To your point, you can't build relationships if you're not able to connect on some very basic social things.

JANICE

And we need money. We need an investment in girls, to let their lives be full, if we really want to transform these kids. That is so critical.

[Sociologist] Mario Small writes about this all the time. He's always doing a social network analysis. And I'm always like, *Mario, this is a network issue!* Who is the central node? It's the kid. So all the nodes around the kid need to be bolstered for that kid to thrive, and that's what I need y'all to see. So unless you're willing to put dollars in all the nodes around her, then this kid is still at risk. And that framework doesn't seem to be [in place], which is why I keep thinking about education as the intersection of community, family, and government.

We have so much happening in many community schools that are able to do better work when we decide that they can be this healing thing. I was really moved by that framing, because I talked about the fact that every good thing that has happened to me has been centered around school. Schools did that for me. So can we get it to do that for 25 million others?

MONIQUE

Right. If you are designing a curriculum, for example, and you are thinking about how to engage the whole student, don't just tokenize Black girls or use frameworks that are inherently racist, that are going to be distracting or hostile to Black children. Black girls will inevitably sense it and say something about it.

JANICE

Even the best, most obedient Black girl is going to be bothered. And if they say nothing, that's the worst. Engendering silence in young people is the worst thing you can do. You want brazen if you want healing and liberation. You need them to articulate what is wrong.

MONIQUE

I agree. One of the things that I hear from girls all the time is that they just want everybody to have Black history. Because we only offer it as an elective for the Black kids, but anti-Black racism thrives outside that space. And now we're hyperaware of it, and have language to identify it, and understand the aggressions—micro and macro. But there has just been an inability for this nation to really come to grips with what is required in our learning spaces around this question of racial literacy. They just don't want to be seen as racist, and that's not enough.

Takeaways for Your Practice

In 2019, 6-year-old Kaia was recorded tearfully pleading with an officer not to arrest her after she experienced a serious moment of dysregulation in school and fell into a violent tantrum. Screaming "help me" after realizing that she was being escorted to a police car, Kaia's incident became another in the string of recorded interactions between Black girls and law enforcement that demonstrate schools' unnecessary overreliance on police officers to respond to children in crisis. Nearly two years later, she reportedly suffered from separation anxiety and a lack of trust in authority. Though the state attorney dropped the charges against her and expunged her record, her grandmother has shared that Kaia—once a joyful child—now has to bring herself out of "despair."[7]

That transformation is not hopeful.

Ultimately our pedagogical practices must reflect an intention to honor the development of all students, wherever they are along their developmental journey. Understanding how society adultifies Black girls provides an opportunity for all of us to develop a stronger commitment to improve our own practices and the biases and considerations that inform how we interact with these girls in schools, communities, and other spaces. Here are ways to help in that process.

Establish a Diversity of Narratives When Seeking to Present the Full Experience of a Community

Do not "teach to the oppression." Elevate what Janice Johnson Dias described in our conversation as "the depth and breadth" of Black humanity. For example, invite the community to share in the storytelling (which helps to establish a welcoming environment) and explore how the school can actively become part of the neighborhood's landscape of joy.

Engage Leadership Skills of Black Girls Throughout the School

Understand advocacy as an important tool for bringing Black girls in closer. Johnson Dias's example of wanting to work with girls whose behaviors may not have made them immediate choices for participation in her program is an important one. Girls who are "loud" and perceived to be aggressive can also be effective leaders when those skills are honed—and when they feel safe around the adult who is working with them. To engage the leadership of Black girls in the school, be sure not to render invisible—or unqualified—those young people who question authority. Often they are questioning authority because they see leadership qualities in themselves and want it recognized by those willing to take the time and make the investment.

Ensure Representation in the Curriculum and Learning Space That Does Not Treat the Experiences and Contributions of Black Girls as "Optional" Learning

Relegating the study of Black girls' experiences to the status of elective signals that they are not necessary learning for all students. Core curricula should include literature, case studies, and other components that include perspectives across the identity spectrums represented by the United States' culturally and linguistically diverse student body—and that includes Black girls.

Honor Art as a Form of Healing, and Use Aspirations to Welcome Black Girls' Thoughts About How to Make Classrooms Joyful Places

Play, dance, and singing in the learning experience play an important role in making school a safe space to recover from trauma. In this effort, be sure to engage Black girls in the following inquiries:

- What makes you happy? How does that show up in your learning style? (No student in K–12 is too young to express how they feel they learn best.)

- What excites you about learning?
- What do you need to be a good learner?
- Who do you need to support your joyful learning?

Additionally, engage educators, school leaders, and developers of educational materials in the following inquiries:

- How are you representing the authentic voices of Black girls in the learning?
- How are you capturing the various learning styles of culturally and linguistically diverse students?
- How are you cultivating accountability around your own biases?
- How do your measures of success include joy?
- What makes your students happy? How do you know this?

5

Building Community Connections That Inspire Black Girl Scholars

As you can imagine, I bled. I bled. After bleeding for a while, I fainted thereafter. . . . I am lucky, I never died, but many die. . . . It was a rusty, old knife, and it was difficult. . . . Three weeks later, I was healed, and I was back in high school. I was so determined to be a teacher now so that I can make a difference in my family.
—Kakenya Ntaiya, TEDxMidAtlantic Talk

Kakenya Ntaiya is an educator among educators. A survivor of female genital mutilation (FGM) and an advocate for its abolition as a harmful practice, she is recognized around the globe for her staunch commitment to the physical, intellectual, and emotional well-being of girls in Kenya, her home. She has inspired millions with her TED talks about building schools for girls as a key strategy to provide a lifetime of opportunity and community transformation.

I met Kakenya in Palm Springs, California, where we were both delivering a talk for TEDWomen. She delivered a powerful talk on the transformative power of education in her life—and the lives of other Maasai girls at risk of FGM and early marriage—and I was enthralled. She spoke of her schools, the Kakenya Centers for Excellence (KCE I and II) and the ways in which the schools are organizing within the community to shift the public consciousness about FGM, early marriage, and the importance of supporting a girl's education. I was immediately curious. What had she learned in her journey to educate girls that could inform our efforts in the United States? How was she able to bring her community along with her in realizing her dream for an equitable educational system that centered girls? How could *her* healing-centered approaches inform *our* healing-centered approaches?

Together with a team of delegates from EMERGE Academy—a program I launched through the National Black Women's Justice Institute with the Mentoring Center, Girls Inc., and the Alameda [California] County Office of Education—I set out to explore the community connections that made the Kakenya Centers for Excellence a reality by visiting two of the campuses in East Africa. Launched by Kakenya's Dream and located in Trans Mara West, Kenya, approximately 250 miles from Nairobi, the two all-girls boarding schools offer a slate of holistic programming alongside academic instruction to educate and prepare girls for growth, leadership, and empowerment in the Maasai villages of Enoosaen and Isampin.

Though separated by continents, as well as varying geopolitical histories, there were shared narratives about surviving histories of oppression at the intersections of race, gender, and age that connected our work. Most important, her success with establishing schools that were designed as locations for healing is a necessary development for the praxis of healing-centered education. For this book, we talked about her work.

MONIQUE

Visiting two of your schools was amazing for our EMERGE team. Honestly, our team had never seen a community in partnership with schools in such a profound, coordinated way. It was really interesting because the most common way we've seen schools engage in partnership with community is simply by inviting parents to come in for scheduled meetings, performances, or fundraisers. It's limited. But I felt like you were able to hold on to something special by engaging partnership as an investment in the girls and their gifts. It actually led to a lot of questions for us.

Let me say that the girls were so giving to us. We asked them at one point to share what they wanted to say to a girl in the United States. And they said things like, *Girls can do anything. You are in charge of yourself. You can move . . .* things like that. Ultimately, we noticed the consistent pattern between what the girls were saying, what the chief was saying, what the elders in the community were saying, what the teachers were saying, and I was like, *Kakenya did her work!* Everybody has all the talking points. [Laughs]

How did you get everybody on the same page? How were you able to make sure everybody is aligned in a way that has centered girls so intentionally?

KAKENYA

It took time. Before we existed, everybody was talking about boys as the leaders. Or *So-and-so's son did well in school.* There was more focus on the boys. We became the *one* school that was focused on girls, and the primary goal for the school was to ensure that girls avoid female genital cutting and also to avoid early marriages. The goal was for girls to go to school and to become something in society. So that was pretty much the mission—as simple as that.

People know that when they go to a Kakenya's Dream school, it's more about them feeling like they have to become something. Not just marriage and not just FGM. So they had these expectations, and we all have the expectation that each girl somehow is going to drive her experiences, and they're going to go beyond what the community may have prescribed for them. And it's taken us 10 years.

They have actually seen the results of each transitional point for the girls. With regard to the national exam in 8th grade, they're all doing very well. When they go to high school, they're continuing. So they have seen the persistence and what we said, and now they can see it for themselves. So it becomes easy because you see it, and the community is involved, and the parents are involved. The teachers have to be involved, and the students have to be involved. That's their goal for coming to the school. It is for that purpose.

MONIQUE

So what does partnership mean, then, for you? How do you make sure that this relationship between schools and the parents and communities isn't just transactional?

KAKENYA

I think at the end of the day, we invested. And the good thing is that we are in the same community, and these kids from the same community are going to the same school, so we speak the same language. We know. We're trying to end the same practices that are going on, and it becomes part of you. So when I was starting the school, people used to call it "that woman thing." Then, when we started seeing the fruits of school and girls did very well, then they started singing the gospel. You know, their fathers started becoming proud. They realized that they were part of making the school successful. I would always—through the parent meetings, any community meetings we have—I would always be asking the chief if this is where we want to go or what he thought. It's about really involving them in the decision making. It can't be transactional, because it's not, really. It's about empowering girls.

All of us know that the community has to play that role. The teachers have to play their role, the girls have to play their role, and everybody has to play that role for us to be successful. So if a parent can't send a girl to school, that means he's not playing his part. If they're going to make sure that they inflict pain through FGM and marry them, they're not playing their part. So everybody has a part to play, and since we all decided that we wanted to create a better future for the girls, it's all of us. It's the ownership, it's the being involved, and it's through the decision making. It cannot be transactional.

MONIQUE

You had a lot of men who had "bought in" and understood what was important. At one point, we had a conversation about how hard it is to sometimes change the ideas of *women* who have been tied to the old ways and who may feel a sense of duty to uphold some of the old ways. How do you get past that? How do you help women understand the need for a shift?

KAKENYA

The women's approach has been really personal, like one-on-one, because we all went through what we went through, and we all want a better future for our children. I think the biggest hindrance for women was not knowing the power they have and thinking that they have to uphold tradition because if they don't, the men would be on their case. Once we brought them together, they could see that if they kept supporting their daughter to go to school, their husband would not beat them.

Or it'll come down to saying, *Look, this is your daughter. Would you want her to live life like you're living? Are you proud?* This may lead a woman to reflect on herself, because we live in a world where we rarely reflect on "us." It's really about one-on-one relationships, and talking and understanding. I know the community very well. I know the people who live there very well. Sometimes people just need to sit down and have coffee or have tea, and just talk. And from that, once you empower one woman, she goes on to be an advocate for another woman. Before you know it, it's a ripple effect.

MONIQUE

So, have you met women who just didn't agree? Or were suspicious of the effort to change the culture? How do you work with the hard ones?

KAKENYA

Yeah. I think the biggest thing is FGM, because we all know the pain, and we all can relate to women dying from childbirth. I would actually be able to talk to them about that specific experience of giving birth and how that was terrifying. So it's kind of like explaining from that end. Then most of them will say, *No one will marry the girl who is not cut.* Then that's when we are like, *OK. That's 18 to 20 years down the line; so why are we talking about it now?*

To me, it's not necessarily about solving the problems immediately. It's more about biting little bits. So if I can win that case for the one girl to keep going to school, then they will start seeing the benefit as they go. So it's like, *If you're worried about FGM, that's not something you should be worried about* now. *You're thinking about them not getting married, but that could be 20 years from now. So for now, we want to help her to go to school, and we want to help her avoid getting married. We want to make sure that she's doing well in school.* Once you put it at the end of education and it's like a positive thing, they start to accept it. Then the girls start advocating for themselves.

At the end, you just need to hold on. You can't create change within a day. I mean, it takes years. And those years are not about coming in to end FGM, or ending early marriages, or empowering this community in a year. It doesn't work like that.

Literally, the first year could just be like, we're having tea and no conversations are happening. We are just creating the space for people to be comfortable, for people to see who is in the room, and to bring new things and people. And it is like, *OK, what are we talking about today?* Then before you know, somebody is creating that space for acceptance and being comfortable. Then we move to being able to go to talk about those other issues. So what you're seeing in my school and community now is this work that we did over time. We have consistently been there, consistently staying here.

The biggest thing with international organizations is that they want to come and have a project for two years. It doesn't work with some of the cultural practices or norms that have been there for generations. It doesn't end by going in there and expecting results in a year. Social change takes time.

MONIQUE

I was actually impressed by the [village] chief, who at one point said that it's his goal to have a thousand Kakenyas. You know, he said he was really impressed. I asked him about men. I asked how we share this message with men. And he said, *We want the best for our daughters, and the goal is to create more Kakenyas.*

KAKENYA

That's great! [Laughs]

MONIQUE

There was an understanding that when you invest in a girl, the village improves, and the community improves. This was a prevalent message that I don't necessarily feel is as resonant in the United States. I think in the United States, because people are so individual with their notion of success, sometimes they get lost in this notion that investing in a girl is also investing in a nation. But it feels like that's been a winning argument for you.

KAKENYA

Absolutely! It's a global message, but I actually took it to the local language. Whenever a woman or a girl in my community goes home for a visit after she is married—when she goes to visit her mother or dad or family—she would always bring sugar. This is a tradition where we always bring sugar and tea leaf. If she had no money, she would actually come with a blanket for you, and when men visit, they don't bring anything. So I would use the same analogy.

A girl is always going back to her home; she's going to check on her parents. She's always there with that emotional connection to the family, while the boy kind of uproots himself and goes on to build his own place. So I really built onto that. I took that and said, *Look, we've educated so many men in this community, but they're all gone. Who have you seen come back to give this opportunity to their people?*

So imagine a million Kakenyas who went back to their communities and did something. It doesn't have to be the same thing I'm doing. It could actually mean giving back to your immediate family. It could be like you're building at your mother's house, or you are investing in your little sister. It's really that minimal way of giving back, which is inside women. It's inside us, and we grow up knowing that whenever you go to somebody's house, you have to bring something. Men don't do that. So when you empower a woman, definitely, she will give back, and it's really investing in the community and investing in the nation.

MONIQUE

Have you thought about what other schools could learn from your model?

KAKENYA

I haven't really spent time on that. Right now we're in the process of actually defining what our replicable model is. What are the things that we can share with others? I think that doing something that is working, and being able to share that with others, would be a great thing. . . . What did *you* learn from your visit that we could share?

MONIQUE

I learned that, number one, your success has a lot to do with how you have effectively been able to organize around the notion that educating a girl is essential to *community development*. And not just educating a girl just for the sake of educating a girl. It was really about how you have the community in line to articulate what the impact is. That is transformative, I think. Bringing the community into the school is a different model, and building out a community council is different. It's a different model than the parent-teacher organizations.

What U.S. schools could learn from your model is how to actively center the voices of elders in the learning process, and to engage elders in a way that is meaningful and that calls on young people to understand their place in the culture. In the United States, we use a lot of "volunteer" structures that are very detached. You come in for two weeks, or you come in for a set amount of time, and then that's it. You're often not invited to bring your full self.

KAKENYA

Yeah.

MONIQUE

But when you do bring your full self, that's when you build the connections that actually are transformative. And those of us who have been volunteers or run schools know that. What you *do* with these relationships is critical.

KAKENYA

We do have deep relationships. That's the big thing that we have invested in over time. And it is important that you do that. They'll literally come into the class and talk to the kids and say things like, *OK, do you have any issues? Is there something I need to talk to the teacher about?* When we have events in the schools, parents have to be very involved. It's not just like, *We give a donation and then things happen.* It's like, *I have to be present to do something. This is for our kids.*

MONIQUE

We had a chance to watch some of the elders, the grandmothers, come in and talk to the girls in your school. We didn't understand what they were saying, but we could see the language and body language of the girls [laughs] and the storytelling of the grandmothers connecting with the girls. I was with my daughter, and one of the grandmothers reminded her of my mother, so she was even into it. She was like, *I don't know what she's saying, but I like her.* [Laughs] So I feel like there's an energy that you're able to capture, that breeds excellence. And that, to me, is ultimately what this is about.

When we were talking to some of the young leaders and prefects, they were very inquisitive. They wanted to know more about where we were from and what some of the opportunities are in the United States. And I think, for them there was this interest in a commitment to excellence that was tied to their commitment to their study, their commitment to community, or for some, their commitment to God and to family—it was all connected. The way that they were really unapologetic about that connection . . . it was beautiful. It led me to start thinking about what happens when Black girls specifically, and girls more generally, are not shy in their gift. I feel like there is a lot of pouring into the gifts of girls at your school. You can see it among the little ones, and you can see it among the older ones.

KAKENYA

That's what they're there for, for us to give them the space to grow within their talents. I always tell the girls, *Each one of us has something to offer the world, and we need to develop that thing, because that's what will make you live longer. That's why you're here.* I think the biggest thing in the societies that we live in is that we are prescribed to be this kind of thing you should *do* instead of just letting them grow within what they're supposed to *be*. You have to figure out the two, and if you don't create the space, then one is going to go away.

MONIQUE

You know, so much of this work is a deep meditation on what happens when girls are not shy in their gift. What do girls give back? Not just what they will physically give, but what else can they give to society, and the school, when we fully pour into them?

Why did you create the school as the place for this transformative work? Why not some other place?

KAKENYA

Because I felt like that is the *only* place I could control. It would take a lot of going to homes to create that. So for us it was like an intervention. Getting that 9-year-old girl into a safe space when society is telling her, *You're a big girl.* We're going to tell her, *You're a child,* you know? She needs to start behaving well. We need to tell her to jump rope. We wanted to cancel what the society will be telling her, and we couldn't do that in an environment that is already doing that to her. So that's why the school was the natural place to create that space.

I sat down with community members. All of my work is about ownership, so I sat down with different groups—you know, fathers, mothers . . . you sit down with the pastors, and you sit down with the motorbike riders. You just sit with groups of people, and then within that, we came up with a committee. Now we're working on how to roll it all out, because if you bring in an outsider, then it becomes the thing for "those people"; it's not *our* thing. If you relate with them, it's really been just the work that we've been doing with the people in the community. A little of the work we do with the girls will bring outsiders, and occasionally a speaker, but they're not the main people. We can bring them in for subject matter reference, ideas, techniques—but the actual work is driven by the people from the community.

MONIQUE

That's a whole different framework, with the work being driven in the community to inform what happens in the school.

KAKENYA

Yeah.

MONIQUE

It's also about leadership. It's about what people are finding attractive. It's about what transformation looks like to the *whole community*.

KAKENYA

You can't just create a space that is too foreign to people. You have to create a space that is relatable. In my 4th grade class, I have tables instead of desks so the girls can sit in circles, because in our community, when people gather, we sit in circles everywhere we go. So that's one of the biggest things. I'm putting familiar spaces together called "sitting areas," or whatever, and this is bringing people together. The cow is part of us so you can't really live without a cow. So we had to have that on campus. You don't even think about it. So there's something good about our culture, but there's also something good about it being present in school. You have to blend the two so that it doesn't look like going to school is bad, that it's going to make you "radical"—because that's the mindset people have. An educated woman is "radical" because she doesn't behave. The belief is that she's promiscuous, she's, you know, all of what society thinks is negative about women. So you have to be able to have a power there, and to be able to go into school. We will say to them, *Oh, yeah, it's our school.* Like, they don't even have to think twice. So the girls will be reminded always that in their community, there's milking the cows. So they come and milk the cow in the evening sometimes. While in our school, they are constantly reminded of their homes, and they are constantly reminded about their people.

People used to say that I'm spoiling the girls, because boarding schools in Kenya don't provide milk. But I provide milk, and the girls love it. And then some weekends, we are like, *OK, time for cooking.* So the girls go cook, and they just make what they want to eat. It should be fun, but you need to bring both because you will need to always be conscious about the other end of the dichotomy, and really creating this new society. That's what we're trying to do.

MONIQUE

How did you get your teachers ready to support this?

KAKENYA

We get teachers from different parts of the country. So the good thing is teachers are not just from the local community. We get them from different parts of the country, and then, of course, we have to retrain them. We do performance evaluations every year—in some cases, every four months. We ask, *How are you doing? How are you performing?*

How is the classroom? Which challenges are you facing? What support do you need? They always hear that from me. I do a lot of programs while I'm on campus, and I'm with the teachers, you know, one-on-one. I go into the classroom to spend time with the girls. If I find an area where they are weak, we talk about it. It's being intentional and purposefully knowing that you have to be there and continue to develop your team, because you can't just develop once and go. You have to *retrain.* They have meetings with their head teachers, and then I come in and evaluate what they did.

MONIQUE

Do they complain about the training, or do they enjoy the training?

KAKENYA

Training is always done at their request. So we'll have planned for three training sessions in a year, and they will tell me, *This is the area we need training in this year,* and *These are the outcomes to which we would know why we are doing the training.* With training that is not effective, we go over it and see how we can improve. We are very open to discussions. We're very relatable. At first, people who come to campus, who didn't know I was Kakenya, were like, *Oh, have you seen Kakenya?* And I was like, *Yeah, just wait a minute. I'll call her.* [Laughs] You'll find me there, and I will be a teacher.

We don't have a hierarchy. I hear a lot about everybody, and I spend time with everybody. Building curriculum, building the team, and inspiring them—that's where we get creative and try things out. It's where I try. . . . Many people are focused on empowering the girls alone, and then you forget that the girl does not try by herself. She needs the community around her, so it's important to work with the teachers. It's important to work with the mothers and fathers, and I think it's important to involve the community in the empowerment of the girl.

Takeaways for Your Practice

There is no doubt that Kakenya Ntaiya has created something special in rural Kenya. The obvious question is, What from this model can be applied to educational systems in the United States?

Consider that Kakenya has mobilized a community to unapologetically center girls in the discourse on educational opportunity. By linking education to the physical well-being of girls, she also crafted a narrative in which education is a public health issue and central to the healing work necessary to support bold futures for girls. In the United States, there is the common assumption that girls uniformly have equal access to a high-quality education, but data reveal that racial disparities among specific measures of success and performance continue to undermine that narrative.

Several aspects in the work of the Kakenya's Dream Centers for Excellence are transferrable to schools in the United States that are seeking to uplift and facilitate the highest possibility among their Black girls. These include the following:

- **Schools are extensions of communities** and cannot be seen as independent entities with no connection to the students being educated inside them.
- **Black girls give back to communities** and therefore define their success in terms of collective well-being, not just individual achievement. When girls thrive, their whole communities thrive.
- **Educators must see themselves as stewards of healing,** not just intellectual educational attainment.
- **School leaders can never lose sight of who they are at their core and why they love education.** A love for learning is infectious and has to be felt by the teachers and staff, as well as the students. Believing in the promise of the girl child is an investment

in girlhood, and it requires the active practice of countering adultification.

Kakenya Ntaiya's model offers inspiration and guidance to schools seeking to counter school pushout among Black girls. It does so in its unapologetic engagement of culture in the pedagogical and climate-related elements of learning—and in the core mission to engage education in the effort to counter trauma and retraumatization.

6

The Path Forward: Elevating Purpose over Punishment

If you get, give. If you learn, teach.

—Maya Angelou

Education is a collaboration between purveyors of information and those seeking to acquire it—but everyone involved should be seekers of *knowledge*. Contrary to how so many of our educational institutions have come to understand and define measures of success, it is not solely the individual accomplishments, or performance on assessments, that indicate whether students are having a positive experience along their educational journey. The fear that has undermined rigorous discussions about racial equity in U.S. public schools must be replaced by a deeper commitment to cultivate high-quality schools as just institutions. Black girls need this, and every other student does too. The conversations in the previous chapters invite educators to explore mechanisms for countering the criminalization of Black girls in schools. These conversations cannot be compartmentalized to the extent that we ignore the political climate informing much of the public debate about race in public schools today.

The Controversy over Critical Race Theory

In the spring of 2021, politically conservative influencers launched a woefully underdeveloped national debate about the relevance of critical race theory in schools.[1] By July 15, 2021, one study found that 26 states had introduced bills or taken other steps to "restrict teaching critical race theory or limit how teachers can discuss racism and sexism."[2] As a result, many organizers and politicians began using the phrase without an understanding of what it is and what it means for the next generation of students.

Critical race theory, or CRT, is a legal framework developed by legal scholars for understanding the historical and sociopolitical context in which contemporary racial bias and discrimination exist. As a theory, it explores racism and the lingering vestiges of enslavement as a critical foundation for developing protections to support the legal, civil, and human rights of Black people and other people of color. Intersectionality is a core framework within the body of CRT scholarship, which demands that we must not only consider how race—and racial bias—affects the experiences of Black people as a protected class, but we must also be aware of how one's other identities (gender, ability, sexuality, etc.) affect relationships with institutions, policies, and the law.[3]

In education, CRT—as advanced by scholars such as Gloria Ladson-Billings—recognizes the omnipresence of racial bias and invites a deeper analysis of how institutions have functioned to perpetuate the structures of inequity and exacerbated harm through what they teach and how they teach it.[4] CRT in education is not—and never has been—a blanket indictment of white people. It is also neither a reversal of what I call "teaching to the oppression" nor a strategy to teach that people of European descent are inherently "bad." It is an acknowledgment of the white supremacist ideology that is woven into the pedagogical practices of institutions tasked to educate all children—particularly public schools in the United States, which are now disproportionately composed of children who are of Black, Latinx, Indigenous and Native, Asian, Pacific Islander, and Arab descent. Carefully curated, school-based discussions about the history of white supremacy and racial violence, as well as the lingering vestiges of structural racism, provide opportunities for learning and healing—for everyone.

Legislative efforts to ban and substantially limit these discussions in K–12 classrooms are essentially banning the teaching of historical facts, which is an assault on critical thinking. For example, in Texas, the 2021 state legislature passed a "critical race theory" bill that limits professional development on topics that rigorously explore strategies to dismantle structural racism and bans explorations of conscious and unconscious bias in schools, among other things. That action presents a significant barrier to academic and social innovation—and a tremendous impediment to building the type of caring learning communities that provide students with the social and intellectual tools they need to navigate global communities with competence and confidence. Schools' capacity to be locations for intellectual and emotional safety—and thus to counter school pushout for Black girls and other students of color—is reduced when we institutionalize, via codification, the notion that the *study* of historical facts that guide intellectual inquiry is problematic.

This type of anti-intellectualism should have no place in schools. A failure to investigate oneself stunts growth. Weaponized, this practice actually facilitates—and locks into place—the structural violence of erasure, the normalization of exploitation, and racialized gender bias that is too familiar to Black girls and their families.

Students of color, and their families, are typically having these discussions anyway; so the only population being sheltered from these discussions is white students. That omission is both a disadvantage and a dangerous proposition in an increasingly diverse, global educational environment and economy. Being a person of color in the United States means that you are typically born into a community conversation about how to understand and protect against racial violence. The practice of mental and physical health in the racially and socially stratified structure of the United States requires that educators, educational policymakers, and curriculum designers become aware of how to cultivate conditions in the learning environment to counter the negative effects that make schools part of the tapestry of harm.

Building Relationships to Embrace the Entire Student

The fundamental theme of my conversations with Venus Evans-Winters, Janice Johnson Dias, and Kakenya Ntaiya about Black girls is that *education must be a practice of teaching to—and learning from—the entire student.* That goal cannot be achieved without an honest discussion about how their identities were shaped by specific ideas about race, gender, sexuality, and other factors in the United States. The relationships we build with and for Black girls to engage them as essential learners require that we prepare to cultivate spaces that acknowledge learning *as we are—*as sacred. Students do not need to be "fixed" in order to learn; they need safety and care. What we do to facilitate a sacred space is radically different than what we do if we are preparing young people for futures of incarceration, criminalization, and surveillance.

So much of how we relay information depends on the relationships that educators have with students. I have concluded from my interactions with young people around the United States that they can learn from us if they feel safe with us. Therefore, the most important takeaway for your practice from the conversations recounted in this book is the understanding that in order to develop meaningful relationships—rooted in understanding—with Black girls, educators and those responsible for the ecosystem in which they are educated must embrace a rigorous commitment to facilitating learning spaces that are not punishment-oriented, but rather healing-centered, joyful, and accountable.

Educators' intent matters as they approach that relationship building. As I have repeated in this book and in other writings on this topic, it is paramount to starve any lingering "savior complex" from feeding on our intentions to improve learning conditions for Black girls. You may have noticed that throughout this book, I elevate more questions than I prescribe answers. I do so because the practice of education is local. How we orchestrate schools that counter the pushout of Black girls depends on the specific conditions in our individual school. Although there are global factors (which I discuss in *Pushout* and *Sing a Rhythm, Dance a Blues*) that inform the collective experiences shared by Black girls in the United States, how these prevailing ideas interact with the specific policies, practices, and conditions in a school will vary. How do we expand the lanes for success in schools such that Black girls can confidently and consistently locate themselves in these spaces is the open inquiry—and it requires educators to think rigorously about how their pedagogical practices and relationships with students provide, rather than restrict, opportunity.

Those who are charged with orchestrating Black girl excellence in their learning environment must be committed to prioritizing purpose over punishment. The emphasis on punishment has produced systems of learning that stifle creativity, undermine the development of critical thinking skills, and prime students for criminalization. Emphasizing purpose allows educators to steer young people—even when they make mistakes—toward their own wisdoms, as both a strategy for healing and a mechanism for learning.

Lessons from Indigenous Africa

Educators can guide Black girls toward their purpose by engaging the indigenous wisdoms that have helped people of African descent recognize their talents amid structural oppression. So we return to Malidoma Somé, who posed the question *What teaches you?* One answer comes from the ancient wisdoms shared by the Dagara people of West Africa, who understand the relationships between five elements (fire, water, earth, mineral, and nature) as representations of characteristics that lead us toward our purpose. According to this particular cosmological belief, people take on the characteristics of an element depending on the year in which they were born.

According to Somé, the Dagara medicine wheel suggests that people who are born in the years associated with fire are connected to the ancestral realm, meaning they are often those who are "at the margins of their culture. They cannot quite fit in, and other people have problems understanding why they won't behave like everyone else." They may be interpreted as "impatient, hyperactive, and sometimes intolerant. A fire person cannot stay idle."[5] Connecting with fire people may require elevating their purpose as individuals who engage their leadership and connection with the world of the spirit and their capacity to provide warmth and comfort when they are deeply connected to their ancestral wisdoms and culture.

Those who are born in the years associated with the element of water may help to balance the "fire" personalities. These are people who may "perceive the world in terms of possibilities. The water person thinks of community, relationship, love, and harmony," but left without nurturing and inspiration, these individuals may also have "little ambition."[6] Elevating the purpose of the water people may include inviting them to provide balance and reconciliation when the environment is dysregulated.

Those who are born in the years associated with earth are likely to be "nurturers who, like all grandmothers, want everybody to feel fed, content, respected, and loved."[7] Earth people may be inclined to give abundantly, and they represent "survival and healing, unconditional love and caring."[8] Working with earth people means recognizing the centrality of their purpose, noticing them as a grounding force in the composition of the community.

Those born in years associated with the mineral element may be inclined to elevate memory and communication. Mineral people understand, intuitively, how to connect with the wisdom of their bones, which are believed to "store thousands of years of information. . . . The person who has a mineral nature speaks a great deal because mineral expresses in discourse what is stored in coded form within the bones. .

. . A mineral person's love for argument, for different ways of saying the same thing, and for eloquent ways of saying nothing can baffle the non-mineral person."[9] Connecting with mineral people involves recognizing their storyteller orientation and potential to remind the collective about their history.

Last, for those born in years associated with nature, change is a way of life. Nature people are inclined to "transformation, mutation, adjustment, flexibility, cyclicality, life, death, and magic. . . . Nature people challenge us to be real, to be ourselves."[10] To build relationships with nature people, we must be willing to present ourselves as authentic and to engage them in their ability to shift. Because play is such an essential communication style for the nature person, educators can reach a nature person through stories, metaphor, and being willing to change themselves.

A unit in balance has a bit of each of these elements and engages them to facilitate reciprocal relationships where community is cultivated and nurtured. Although the cosmological beliefs of the Dagara people are fascinating to me, I am not suggesting that educators necessarily adopt those beliefs. However, I am suggesting that by engaging young people in conversations about how their educational journey connects to their *purpose* and how they can uplift their skills as tools to realize their purpose, we can engage them with love and appreciation rather than fear.

Elevating purpose over punishment is how schools increase their capacity to be locations for healing. If, for example, a girl is loquacious—to the point of disruption—it might be helpful to know that she is a storyteller. If a girl is a fighter, it might be helpful to know that she is a survivor. If a girl keeps interfering in scenarios that involve another person being harmed (real or perceived), knowing that she is seeking balance is important. Seeing girls through a lens of purpose allows educators to build relationships—and interventions—that move toward healing and that widen the gates for learning and growth. Educators and learning institutions must engage new tools to unlock new possibilities.

Addressing the Challenge

Ultimately, the reflections I have shared in this book via conversations with Janice Johnson Dias, Venus Evans-Winters, and Kakenya Ntaiya reveal that schools must be so much more than a building with bodies inside it. My conversations with these women have also revealed that when educators bring to their practice an understanding of the complexities of living in a Black girl body, they can engage their peers in a rigorous approach to education as a liberative tool. Our discussions about what it means to support Black girls in their gifts suggests a broader question about how we actively challenge the tropes and stereotypes about Black girlhood (e.g., as sassy, combative, loud) that limit our understanding of how these girls and femmes are trying to navigate their lives—including their learning environment.

Much of how the public consciousness constructs Black girlhood is through a lens of deficiency or superhumanity. Our goal as educators must always be to recognize Black girls as developing young minds and bodies that reflect curiosity, humor, joy, and resilience. These are gifts—even if they initially manifest in problematic ways. Our work is to teach them, as we do other students, ways of learning about themselves as they learn academic content. School pushout is the result of educators—and others in the educational space—failing to support Black girls in their gifts.

Supporting Black girls in their gifts requires educators to engage a series of specific directions with their practices, including the following:

- **Create or increase capacity for inclusive, systemic educational justice,** even if Black girls are academically excelling under the current conditions. Increasing capacity here means exploring the school rules, policies, and practices (and sometimes personnel) that unfairly target or punish Black girls and other students of color because of cultural norms. For example, policies that restrict or that specifically ban Afros, locs, and hair extensions will disproportionately target Black girls. Dress code policies that leave room for subjective interpretation of what is provocative will disproportionately and unfairly target Black girls. School codes of conduct or state laws that punish expressions that include elevated volume, congregating in groups, speaking up, or recording incidents of police use of force are examples of policies rooted in fear—and reflect a gross negligence with respect to understanding normal adolescent development.

- **Counter the adultification of Black girls in schools.** We can do this by actively humanizing them and engaging them in articulating how their girlhood is being supported by the school—in the curriculum, in school-based functions, and in extracurricular activities. Adultification strips Black girls of the ability to express themselves using a range of emotions without the threat of harsh punishment or reprimand. It renders them vulnerable to discipline instead of nurturing and comfort. Adultification removes Black girls' ability to process and heal from trauma; it assumes that they can handle harm without support and facilitates adults' inability to recognize signs of trauma in the first place. Acknowledging trauma is different than pathologizing Black girlhood, so it is important not to conflate the two. Black girlhood is a beautiful experience filled with creativity, curiosity, boldness, and love. However, public constructs of it distort these qualities to render Black girls vulnerable to an oppressive gaze that denies them the opportunity to show their peers and educators who they actually are, rather than what people expect them to be.

- **Develop systems of analysis for your own educational content and teaching practice that honor the intention to be actively antiracist.** Because racism is fundamentally about power rather than merely about bias or bigotry, it is important to explore what guides your use of power in the classroom. What ideas inform your decisions about Black girls? What accountability measures have you established to ensure that Black girls and their peers can feel emotionally and intellectually safe in your classroom? How are you ensuring that the measures you take are rooted not in saviorism but rather in a genuine appreciation for the capacity and promise of Black girls, alongside other students of color?

As I mentioned in the first chapter of this book, Martin Luther King Jr. invited us to view justice as "power correcting everything that stands against love." By extension, educational justice is the use of power in learning environments to correct what stands against love. As I stated at the onset of this book, the policies, practices, conditions, and prevailing consciousness that facilitate school-to-confinement pathways for Black girls are rooted in fear. Zero-tolerance policies are rooted in fear. An increase in school policing and an overreliance on law enforcement officers and other instruments of surveillance are rooted in fear. Apathy or disregard toward Black students who are struggling in school is rooted in fear. The absence of meaningful relationships between students and teachers is rooted in fear. Each of these facilitates school pushout and undermines schools as locations for learning.

In contrast, building meaningful relationships with Black girls is rooted in love. Providing spaces for them to convene in safe affinity groups to process and grow from their collective experiences is rooted in love. Engaging them fully as learners in the school is rooted in love. Providing opportunities for them to learn from their mistakes—if or when they make them—rather than discarding them is rooted in love.

In addition to the broader questions that accompany efforts to orchestrate an end to school pushout for Black girls, educators might organize workshops to examine the following specific questions and considerations:

- What is one example of when my actions toward Black girls reflected fear?

Notes: _____

_____

- Why did I respond this way?

Notes: _____

_____

- What was the outcome?

Notes: _____

_____

- Am I satisfied with the response? Explain why or why not.

Notes: _____

_____

- How could my actions in the previous example have been rooted in love instead?

Notes: _____

_____

- What would have been the desired response from this interaction?

Notes: _____

_____

- Overall, how would I describe my relationships with Black girl students?

Notes: _____

_____

- How much do I rely on hearsay or stereotypes about Black girls when interacting with them at my school? What information does this provide? What information does this not provide?

Notes: _____

_____

- What is a first step I can take to improve my relationships with Black girls on campus so that I can rely more on my personal interactions with them rather than what others may tell me?

Notes: _____

_____

- How do my course's learning objectives and lesson plans provide for the visibility of joy among Black girls and women?

Notes: _____

_____

- What is one example of when my interactions with Black girl students reflected a strong and caring relationship?

Notes: _____

_____

- What worked in this interaction? Why did it work?

Notes: _____

_____

- How can I replicate what worked in similar scenarios?

Notes: _____

_____

- How can I build my own capacity (e.g., what classes, books, videos) or network (e.g., group of teachers, volunteers) to respond with care whenever one of my Black girls seems dysregulated and may be facing disciplinary action?

Notes: _____

_____

- How can I rely less on school-based law enforcement or security personnel when Black girls seem to be dysregulated? Removing law enforcement or security from the scenario, who would I want to involve?

Notes: _____

_____

- Who do I need to communicate with in my school to ensure that our professional development and other training opportunities prepare me for my interactions with dysregulated students in noncriminalizing ways?

Notes: _____

_____

- How can our school-based activities and curriculum avoid shrinking or tokenizing the experiences and contributions of Black girls and women?

Notes: _____

_____

- How can my school connect with students and parents to develop codes of conduct that do not encourage the policing of Black girls' bodies and cultural traditions?

Notes: _____

_____

- Who must partner with me to start a conversation at my school about what may be facilitating school pushout among Black girls— and how do we address it?

Notes: _____

_____

These are questions that should be explored and revisited over time, and each of them leads back to what was the first—and what will be the final question, and call to action, of this book: How will you use your power?

Acknowledgments

I start my acknowledgments by thanking my ancestors and elders, whose journeys continue to inform my purpose on this earth. To my mother Katie Couvson, your unwavering support always gives me the strength to move forward. I would also like to thank my daughters Ebony and Mahogany, who have demonstrated grace and understanding for their mother, who is perpetually seeking ways to expand the village of care for Black girls and other girls of color. To my sister Dominique Fulling, thank you so much for helping me organize transcripts. You are always there when I need you. To my sister Yvette Couvson, your song for *Sing a Rhythm, Dance a Blues* helped to inspire some of the thinking for this project. To my brothers Donte Couvson and Xavier Couvson, I love you. To my sister Felicia Bailey-Carr, your commitment to learning as a school leader inspires me. Family, thank you!

It may go without saying that since 2020, U.S. schools—and the educators and children who work in and attend these institutions—have experienced some of the most challenging conditions of the century. The COVID-19 pandemic was not only a global health challenge, but also a shared trauma that disproportionately impacted communities of color due to the legacy of medical racism, misinformation, and structural inequities that predisposed people of color to conditions that placed them at elevated risk of contracting the disease. Schools were thrust into remote learning, relying on technology that was inconsistently available, amid the uncertainty and fear that accompany a new deadly disease. For girls of color and their communities, navigating these conditions amid the ongoing racial violence and trauma that brought public protest to a peak in the summer of 2020 meant that girls of color, particularly Black girls, were thrust into deep vulnerability. In 2020, I also experienced a significant life change and stepped into a new position in philanthropy, which required organization building and the development of an urgent effort to resource the unique needs of girls and femmes of color across the country. The patience of my literary agent, Marie Brown, and the editorial team at ASCD, especially Susan Hills, during this tumultuous time was so deeply appreciated. Thank you!

This book would not have been possible without the many educators who have been willing to conference with me, honestly wrestle through hard questions with me (and each other)—in person and by videoconference. I offer a special embrace to the three scholars who were willing to sit with me and share their brilliant insights for this book. Thank you, Janice Johnson Dias, Venus Evans-Winters, and Kakenya Ntaiya—I am so grateful for all that you bring to the world. Thank you!

Lastly, I wish to extend my deepest gratitude to my sorors of Delta Sigma Theta Sorority, Inc. You all are my rock. I am always so grateful for my community that supports me and my vision for this work, especially my New York–based loved ones, who were by my side while working through the material for this book. A special shout-out to the team at Grantmakers for Girls of Color and the #1Billion4BlackGirls Campaign—you all are the best. There is no other community with whom I'd rather mobilize resources for girls and femmes of color. Let's continue to do this!

Resources

Abolitionist Teaching Network

https://abolitionistteachingnetwork.org/

The Abolitionist Teaching Network is a growing network of educators who are developing and supporting those in the struggle for educational liberation by using the intellectual work and direct action of abolitionists in many forms.

Georgetown Law Center on Poverty and Inequality

https://genderjusticeandopportunity.georgetown.edu/

The Georgetown Law Center on Poverty and Inequality operates the Initiative on Gender Justice and Opportunity, which conducts research to support informed public policies and decision making in schools regarding discipline and responses to girls of color. In addition to its work on adultification, the initiative has produced research on national trends regarding discipline and the impact of restorative approaches to girls of color in schools.

Girls for Gender Equity

www.ggenyc.org/

Girls for Gender Equity (GGE) is an intergenerational organization committed to the physical, psychological, social, and economic development of girls and women. Through education, organizing, and physical fitness, GGE encourages communities to remove barriers and create opportunities for girls and women to live self-determined lives. It envisions a society with optimal physical, economic, educational, and social systems to foster the growth and fulfillment of all its members. To that end, GGE provides programs that develop strengths, skills, and self-sufficiency in girls and women and help them make meaningful choices in their lives with minimum opposition and maximum community support. It organizes campaigns to achieve safety and equality in the social, political, educational, athletic, economic, health, and media worlds of the smaller and larger communities in which girls and women live and work.

GrassROOTS Community Foundation

https://grassrootscommunityfoundation.org/

Founded by Janice Johnson Dias, the GrassROOTS Community Foundation is a public health and social action organization that funds, supports, and develops community programming for women and girls

Monford Dent Consulting

www.monforddentconsulting.com/

Tyffani Monford Dent is a licensed psychologist, author, and nationally recognized presenter on a wide range of topics, including adolescent mental health, social-emotional intelligence in educational settings, and empowering women through emotional-wellness work. Dent provides mental health training and is widely sought after to provide technical assistance on culturally informed mental health services, gender-responsive treatment, the school-to-prison pipeline and Black girls, educating Black girls in white spaces, intersectionality, and social justice work throughout the United States. She has been featured on local and national news programs addressing the importance of emotional wellness in Black communities, mental health in times of national crisis, and the school-to-prison pipeline's impact on Black girls.

National Black Women's Justice Institute (NBWJI)

www.nbwji.org/

The National Black Women's Justice Institute conducts research on, elevates, and educates the public about innovative, community-led solutions to address the criminalization of Black women and girls. The organization aims to dismantle the racist and patriarchal U.S. criminal-legal system and build, in its place, pathways to opportunity and healing. It envisions a society that respects, values, and honors the humanity of Black women and girls, takes accountability for the harm it has inflicted, and recognizes that real justice is healing. The organization provides technical assistance to school districts and schools to interrupt school-to-confinement pathways for Black girls and other girls of color.

National Women's Law Center

https://nwlc.org/let-her-learn/

The National Women's Law Center leads legal advocacy efforts anchored in their series *Let Her Learn*, which provides tools, research, and legal support to address school pushout.

Planet Venus Institute

www.planetvenusinstitute.com

Founded by Venus Evans-Winters, the Planet Venus Institute is an information and resource hub for scholarship, coaching, counseling, and technical assistance associated with supporting the well-being of Black women and girls.

Notes

Chapter 1: The Framework

1. Morris, M. W. (2016). *Pushout: The criminalization of Black girls in schools*. New Press.

2. National Crittenton. (2020). Preliminary summary of themes from *In solidarity conversations: Girls and gender-expansive young people of color respond to COVID-19, economic crisis, and social unrest*, p. 3.

3. Georgetown Law Center on Poverty and Inequality. (2020). *Data snapshot: 2017–2018 national data on school discipline by race and gender*. https://genderjusticeandopportunity.georgetown.edu/wp-content/uploads/2020/12/National-Data-on-School-Discipline-by-Race-and-Gender.pdf

4. Georgetown Law Center on Poverty and Inequality. (2020). *Data snapshot: 2017–2018 national data on school discipline by race and gender*. https://genderjusticeandopportunity.georgetown.edu/wp-content/uploads/2020/12/National-Data-on-School-Discipline-by-Race-and-Gender.pdf

5. *Adultification* refers to the reading of Black girl behaviors as more "adultlike"—what I have described as an age compression that leads adults to perceive that Black girls are more mature than their white counterparts. Research by Jamilia Blake on adultification bias and Black girls has shown that Black girls experience adult perceptions that lead to the belief that they need less nurturing, comfort, and protection than their white counterparts. Adultification bias begins when Black girls are as young as age 5 and peaks when they are between the ages of 10 and 14. See Blake, J., Epstein, R., & González, T. (2017, July). *Girlhood interrupted: The erasure of Black girls' childhood*. Georgetown Law Center on Poverty and Inequality. https://ssrn.com/abstract=3000695

6. Morris, M. W. (2019). *Sing a rhythm, dance a blues: Education for the liberation of Black and Brown girls*. New Press, p. 45.

7. Van der Kolk, B. (2014). *The body keeps the score: Brain, mind, and body in the healing of trauma*. Penguin, p. 38.

8. Morris, M. W. (2019). *Sing a rhythm, dance a blues: Education for the liberation of Black and Brown girls*. New Press.

9.   Cooperative inquiry is part of the family of participatory action research that engages human participants in collaboration with others to explore a topic. It is essentially using a cyclical method of inquiry and action to conduct research *with* rather than *on* people. See Heron, J. (1996). *Co-operative inquiry: Research into the human condition.* SAGE. See also Reason, P., & Heron, J. (1995). Co-operative inquiry, in R. Harre, J. A. Smith, & L. Van Langenhove (Eds.), *Rethinking psychology.* SAGE.

10.   Heron, J. (1996). *Co-operative inquiry: Research into the human condition.* SAGE.

11.   See Morris, M. W. (2016). *Pushout: The criminalization of Black girls in schools.* New Press; Morris, M. W. (2019). *Sing a rhythm, dance a blues: Education for the liberation of Black and Brown girls.* New Press. See also Girls for Gender Equity. (2017). *The schools girls deserve.* https://www.ggenyc.org/the-schools-girls-deserve; and the National Women's Law Center. (2018). *Dress coded: Black girls, bodies, and bias in DC schools.* https://nwlc.org/resources/dresscoded/

12.   Harris, N. (2011). *Writing at the crossroads: Black world essays.* One World Archives Press, p. 120.

13.   Harris, N. (2011). *Writing at the crossroads: Black world essays.* One World Archives Press.

14.   See Jacobs, C. E. (2020). *Ready to lead: Leadership supports and barriers for Black and Latinx girls.* Girls Leadership. https://cdn.girlsleadership.org/app/uploads/2020/07/GirlsLeadership_ReadytoLeadReport.pdf. See also Richardson, E. (2002, June). "To protect and serve": African American female literacies. *College Composition and Communication, 53*(4), 675–704.

15.   See Love, B. L. (2019). *We want to do more than survive: Abolitionist teaching and the pursuit of educational freedom.* Beacon Press.

16.   King Jr., M. L. (1967). *Where do we go from here?* Beacon Press.

17.   Deliso, M., & Ghebremedhin, S. (2021, January 30). Florida teen body-slammed by school resource officer "traumatized," family says. *ABC News.* https://abcnews.go.com/US/florida-teen-body-slammed-school-resource-officer-traumatized/story?id=75582344

18.   See Morris, M. W. (2019). *Sing a rhythm, dance a blues: Education for the liberation of Black and Brown girls.* New Press. See also van der Kolk, B. A. (2014). *The body keeps the score: Brain, mind, and body in the healing of trauma.* Penguin Books; González, T., & Epstein, R. (2021). *Building foundations of health and wellbeing in school: A study of restorative practice and girls of color.* Initiative on Gender Justice and Opportunity, Georgetown Law Center on Poverty and Inequality. https://genderjusticeandopportunity.georgetown.edu/wp-content/uploads/2021/05/21_COPI_BuildingFoundations_Report_Accessible_Final.pdf; and Wachtel, T. & Mirsky, L., (Eds.). (2008). *Safe, saner schools: Restorative practices in education.* International Institute for Restorative Practices.

19.   Delpit, L. (2006). *Other people's children: Cultural conflict in the classroom.* New Press, p. 31.

Chapter 2: Getting Started

1. See https://www.census.gov/quickfacts/newarkcitynewjersey

2. Love, B. L. (2019). *We want to do more than survive: Abolitionist teaching and the pursuit of educational freedom.* Beacon Press, p. 1.

3. See Crenshaw, K. (1991, July). Mapping the margins: Intersectionality, identity politics, and violence against women of color. *Stanford Law Review, 43*(6), 1241–1299.

4. See Bradbury, H. (2015). *The SAGE handbook of action research* (3rd ed.). SAGE. See also Kahane, A. (2012). *Transformative scenario planning: Working together to change the future.* Berrett-Koehler.

Chapter 3: Grieving the Harms of Institutionalized Bias to Cultivate a Righteous Learning Environment

1. Somé, M. P. (1998). *The healing wisdom of Africa: Finding life purpose through nature, ritual, and community.* Penguin Putnam, p. 22.

2. Somé, M. P. (1998). *The healing wisdom of Africa: Finding life purpose through nature, ritual, and community.* Penguin Putnam, p. 55.

3. Gregory, C. (n.d.). The five stages of grief: An examination of the Kübler-Ross model. *Psycom.* https://www.psycom.net/depression.central.grief.html. See also Kübler-Ross, E. (1969). *On death and dying.* Macmillan.

4. Evans-Winters explored this further in her book *Teaching Black Girls,* where she states "When one includes gender, race, and class in [the analysis of community characteristics that foster resilience], the characteristics will inevitably look different [to include]: availability of social organizations that provide cultural and gender-specific resources (e.g., childcare); consistent expression of social norms for desirable behavior (e.g., abstinence or condom use); and opportunities for girls to participate as active societal or community change agents (e.g., opportunities for leadership skills). The conceptualization of resilience will be changed, once multiple (oppressed) identities are added to the analysis" (p. 44).

5. Frantz Fanon's presentation of the psychopathology produced by colonialism and racial hierarchy involves a detailed analysis of the "arsenal of complexes that has been developed by the colonial environment" (*Black Skin, White Masks,* p. 30). This analysis fundamentally attributes the conditioning of Black people's aspirations to achieve "whiteness" or "white-approval" (p. 51). "Cultural hierarchy," he argues, is ingrained into the psyche of Black people, which impacts the thoughts and behaviors of those who experience "systemized oppression" (*The Fanon Reader,* p. 20).

6. See Akala, A. (2020, September 23). *Cost of racism: U.S. economy lost $16 trillion because of discrimination, bank says.* NPR. https://www.npr.org/sections/live-updates-protests-for-racial-justice/2020/09/23/916022472/cost-of-racism-u-s-economy-lost-16-trillion-because-of-discrimination-bank-says

7. Felitti, V. J., Anda, R. F., Nordenberg, D., Williamson, D. F., Spitz, A. M., Edwards, V., Koss, M. P., & Marks, J. S. (1998). Relationship of childhood abuse and household dysfunction to many of the leading causes of death in adults: The adverse childhood experiences (ACE) study. *American Journal of Preventative Medicine 14*(4), 245–258.

8. H.R. 2248, the Ending Punitive, Unfair, School-Based Harm that is Overt and Unresponsive to Trauma (PUSHOUT) Act was reintroduced in 2021 by Representative Ayanna Pressley (D-Massachusetts) to improve schools' capacity to respond to girls of color and other students disproportionately affected by exclusionary discipline. The bill calls for an increase in investments that would create safe and nurturing school environments for all students by (1) establishing $2.5 billion in new federal grants to support states and schools that commit to ban unfair and discriminatory school discipline practices and improve school climates; (2) protecting the Civil Rights Data Collection (CRDC) and strengthening the Department of Education's (ED) Office of Civil Rights (OCR); and (3) establishing a Federal Interagency Taskforce to End School Pushout and examine its disproportionate impact on girls of color.

9. Epstein, R., Blake, J., & González, T. (2017). *Girlhood interrupted: The erasure of Black girls' childhood*. Washington, DC: Georgetown Law Center on Poverty and Inequality. https://ssrn.com/abstract=3000695

10. Dahl, R. E., Allen, N. B., Wilbrecht, L., & Suleiman, A. B. (2018, February 21). Importance of investing in adolescence from a developmental science perspective. *Nature, 554*(7693): 441–450.

11. See Girls for Gender Equity. (2017.) *The schools girls deserve.* https://www.ggenyc.org/the-schools-girls-deserve/

12. See Camera, L. (2017, May 9). Black girls are twice as likely to be suspended, in every state. *U.S. News & World Report.* https://www.usnews.com/news/education-news/articles/2017-05-09/black-girls-are-twice-as-likely-to-be-suspended-in-every-state

13. National Women's Law Center. (2018). *Dress coded: Black girls, bodies, and bias in DC schools.* https://nwlc.org/resources/dresscoded/

14. See González, T., & Epstein, R. (2021). *Building foundations of health and wellbeing in school: A study of restorative practices and girls of color.* Initiative on Gender Justice and Opportunity, Georgetown Law Center on Poverty and Inequality. https://genderjusticeandopportunity.georgetown.edu/wp-content/uploads/2021/05/21_COPI_BuildingFoundations_Report_Accessible_Final.pdf

15. Ohlson, B., & Bedrossian, K. (2016). *Valuing girls' voices: Lived experiences of girls of color in Oakland Unified School District.* Alliance for Girls, with Bright Research Group, p. 13. https://www.brightresearchgroup.com/wp-content/uploads/2018/10/valuing-girls-voices-the-lived-experiences-of-girls-of-color-in-ousd.pdf

16. Breen, K. (2021, May 13). "I felt humiliated": High school student made to cut hair during softball game. *Today.com.* https://www.today.com/news/north-carolina-student-made-cut-hair-during-softball-game-t218264

17. The term *misogynoir*, coined by Moya Bailey, refers to "the ways anti-Black and misogynistic representation shape broader ideas about Black women, particularly in visual culture and digital spaces." See Bailey, M. (2021). *Misogynoir transformed: Black women's digital resistance.* NYU Press.

Chapter 4: Pulling Black Girls in to Orchestrate a Joyful Space

1. See the GrassROOTS website: https://grassrootscommunityfoundation.org/

2. Dias, M., with S. McGowan. (2018). *Marley Dias gets it done: And so can you!* Scholastic, pp. 29–30.

3. See Jacobs, C. (2020). *Ready to lead: Leadership supports and barriers for Black and Latinx girls.* Girls Leadership. https://cdn.girlsleadership.org/app/uploads/2020/07/GirlsLeadership_ReadytoLeadReport.pdf

4. Dias, M., with S. McGowan. (2018). *Marley Dias gets it done: And so can you!* Scholastic, p. 45.

5. In 2020 I visited the Supergirl camp with actor Monique Coleman and spoke to the girls about my journey as an author, educator, filmmaker, and advocate for Black girls.

6. EMERGE (Educating, Mentoring, Empowering, and Reaffirming our Girls for Excellence) is an educational reentry program for girls and femmes in Alameda County. The program is operated by the Mentoring Center, in partnership with the Alameda County Office of Education and Girls, Inc. See http://mentor.org/emerge/

7. Ardrey, T. (2021, March 17). Kaia Rolle was arrested at school when she was 6. Nearly two years later, she still "has to bring herself out of despair." *Yahoo! News.* https://news.yahoo.com/kaia-rolle-arrested-school-she-184755567.html

Chapter 6: The Path Forward

1. See Sawchuk, S. (2021, May 18). What is critical race theory, and why is it under attack? *Education Week.* https://www.edweek.org/leadership/what-is-critical-race-theory-and-why-is-it-under-attack/2021/05

2. *Education Week.* (2021, July 30). Map: Where critical race theory is under attack. https://www.edweek.org/policy-politics/map-where-critical-race-theory-is-under-attack/2021/06

3. Crenshaw, K., Gotanda, N., Peller, G., & Thomas, K. (Eds.). (1996). *Critical race theory: The key writings that formed the movement.* New Press.

4. Ladson-Billings, G. (1998). Just what is critical race theory and what's it doing in a nice field like education? *International Journal of Qualitative Studies in Education, 11*(1), 7–24.

5. Somé, M. P. (1998). *The healing wisdom of Africa: Finding life purpose through nature, ritual, and community.* Penguin Putnam, p. 170.

6. Somé, M. P. (1998). *The healing wisdom of Africa: Finding life purpose through nature, ritual, and community.* Penguin Putnam, p. 172.

7. Somé, M. P. (1998). *The healing wisdom of Africa: Finding life purpose through nature, ritual, and community.* Penguin Putnam, p. 174.

8. Somé, M. P. (1998). *The healing wisdom of Africa: Finding life purpose through nature, ritual, and community.* Penguin Putnam, p. 173.

9. Somé, M. P. (1998). *The healing wisdom of Africa: Finding life purpose through nature, ritual, and community.* Penguin Putnam, pp. 177–178.

10. Somé, M. P. (1998). *The healing wisdom of Africa: Finding life purpose through nature, ritual, and community.* Penguin Putnam, pp. 179–180.

Index

The letter *f* following a page number denotes a figure.

About the Author

 **Monique W. Morris,** EdD, is an award-winning author and social justice scholar with more than three decades of experience in the areas of education, civil rights, and juvenile and criminal justice. She is the president and CEO of Grantmakers for Girls of Color (G4GC), a national philanthropic intermediary that cultivates and mobilizes resources specifically in support of girls, femmes, and gender-expansive youth who identify as Black, Indigenous, Latina, Asian, Arab, Pacific Islander, and other people of color in the United States. Under her leadership, G4GC manages four signature funds: the Love Is Healing Fund, the New Songs Rising Initiative for Indigenous Girls, the Holding a Sister Initiative for Trans Girls of Color, and the Black Girl Freedom Fund, as part of the #1Billion4BlackGirls campaign, which is seeking to mobilize $1 billion in investments centering Black girls over the next 10 years.

Morris is an executive producer and cowriter of the documentary film *Pushout: The Criminalization of Black Girls in Schools* (see www .pushoutfilm.com), which is based on two of her books: *Sing a Rhythm, Dance a Blues: Education for the Liberation of Black and Brown Girls* (New Press, 2019) and *Pushout: The Criminalization of Black Girls in Schools* (New Press, 2016). She is also the author of *Black Stats: African Americans by the Numbers in the Twenty-First Century* (New Press, 2014)

and *Too Beautiful for Words* (MWM Books, 2012); and she worked with Kemba Smith on her book *Poster Child: The Kemba Smith Story* (IBJ Book Publishing, 2011). She has written dozens of articles, book chapters, and other publications on social justice issues and has lectured widely on research, policies, and practices associated with improving juvenile/criminal justice, educational, and socioeconomic conditions for girls and women of color. Her 2018 TED talk on how to stop the criminalization of Black girls in schools has received more than 1.9 million views and been translated into 20 languages.

Morris is the founder and board chair of the National Black Women's Justice Institute (NBWJI), which engages in research, training, and technical assistance to educate the public about innovative, community-led solutions to address the criminalization of Black women and girls. She served as an adjunct associate professor at Saint Mary's College of California from 2013 to 2018 and has taught at the University of San Francisco and California State University, Sacramento. She is a 2012 Soros Justice Fellow; the former vice president for economic programs, advocacy, and research at the National Association for the Advancement of Colored People (NAACP); and the former director of research for the Thelton E. Henderson Center for Social Justice at the UC Berkeley School of Law. She has also partnered with and served as a consultant for federal, state, and county agencies; national academic and research institutions; and communities throughout the United States to develop research, comprehensive approaches, and training curricula to eliminate racial/ethnic and gender disparities in justice and educational systems. Her work in this area has informed the development and implementation of improved culturally competent and gender-responsive services for youth.

Morris's work has been profiled by MSNBC, CSPAN2, the *Washington Post,* the *New York Times,* NPR, and PBS, among other national and local media outlets. Her research intersects race, gender, education, and justice to explore the ways in which Black communities, and other communities of color, are uniquely affected by social policies. She also frequently lectures on the life and legacy of the artist Prince.

Morris can be found on these social media platforms:

- Twitter: @MoniqueWMorris
- Instagram: monique.w.morris
- Facebook: MoniqueWMorrisEdD

Related ASCD Resources

At the time of publication, the following resources were available (ASCD stock numbers in parentheses).

Becoming the Educator They Need: Strategies, Mindsets, and Beliefs for Supporting Male Black and Latino Students by Robert Jackson (#119010)

Building Equity: Policies and Practices to Empower All Learners by Dominique Smith, Nancy Frey, Ian Pumpian, and Douglas Fisher (#117031)

Cultural Competence Now: 56 Exercises to Help Educators Understand and Challenge Bias, Racism, and Privilege by Vernita Mayfield (#118043)

The Equity and Social Justice Education 50: Critical Questions for Improving Opportunities and Outcomes for Black Students by Baruti K. Kafele (#121060)

Even on Your Worst Day, You Can Be a Student's Best Hope by Manny Scott (#117077)

The Innocent Classroom: Dismantling Racial Bias to Support Students of Color by Alexs Pate (#120025)

Keeping It Real and Relevant: Building Authentic Relationships in Your Diverse Classroom by Ignacio Lopez (#117049)

For up-to-date information about ASCD resources, go to www.ascd.org. You can search the complete archives of *Educational Leadership* at www.ascd.org/el.

ASCD myTeachSource®
Download resources from a professional learning platform with hundreds of research-based best practices and tools for your classroom at http://myteachsource.ascd.org/

For more information, send an email to member@ascd.org; call 1-800-933-2723 or 703-578-9600; send a fax to 703-575-5400; or write to Information Services, ASCD, 2800 Shirlington Road, Suite 1001, Arlington, VA 22206 USA.

ascd
whole child

The ASCD Whole Child approach is an effort to transition from a focus on narrowly defined academic achievement to one that promotes the long-term development and success of all children. Through this approach, ASCD supports educators, families, community members, and policymakers as they move from a vision about educating the whole child to sustainable, collaborative actions.

Cultivating Joyful Learning Spaces for Black Girls relates to the **safe** tenet.

For more about the ASCD Whole Child approach,
visit **www.ascd.org/wholechild.**

WHOLE CHILD
TENETS

1 **HEALTHY**
Each student enters school healthy and learns about and practices a healthy lifestyle.

2 **SAFE**
Each student learns in an environment that is physically and emotionally safe for students and adults.

3 **ENGAGED**
Each student is actively engaged in learning and is connected to the school and broader community.

4 **SUPPORTED**
Each student has access to personalized learning and is supported by qualified, caring adults.

5 **CHALLENGED**
Each student is challenged academically and prepared for success in college or further study and for employment and participation in a global environment.